CAN YOU AFFORD TO GROW OLD?

SOLVING THE CRISIS OF MONEY AND HEALTHCARE IN RETIREMENT AND OLD AGE

JAMES P.
ADDICOTT

CHARLES F.
BUTLER

PROBUS PUBLISHING COMPANY
Chicago, Illinois
Cambridge, England

This publication is designed to provide accurate and authoritative information in regard to the subject matter covered. It is sold with the understanding that the publisher is not engaged in rendering legal, accounting or other professional service.

Authorization to photocopy items for internal or personal use, or the internal or personal use of specific clients, is granted by PROBUS PUBLISHING COMPANY, provided that the US$7.00 per page fee is paid directly to Copyright Clearance Center, 27 Congress Street, Salem MA 01970, USA. For those organizations that have been granted a photocopy license by CCC, a separate system of payment has been arranged. The fee code for users of the Transactional Reporting Service is: 1-55738-420-7/92/$0.00 + $7.00

ISBN 1-55738-420-7

Printed in the United States of America

BB

1   2   3   4   5   6   7   8   9   0

Table of Contents

Preface

Two fundamental concerns of every member of our society are money and health care. Few understand the rules under which wealth is obtained or under which health care is provided. Wall Street analysts say that in seeking these two necessities that we are driven by two emotions—greed and fear. Greed drives us to seek the greatest possible return on our investment dollar. Fear often drives us to sell those same assets at a loss if we become wary that a more devastating loss is possible. But selling into a maelstrom often maximizes loss as the doorway becomes too narrow to emit investors with their wealth.

Greed and fear are powerful motivators because most people recognize their own mortality. Whether we admit it, we know that as we age that there will be a period of limited or no productivity. We dream of these days as the "golden age"—when we can retire and enjoy the fruits of our labor. Few people visualize themselves in decrepit old age laboring in a sweat shop to provide meager provisions for themselves or a needy spouse. Fewer people realize that it would be even worse to have that life of impoverished deprivation without a sweat shop in which to toil. Throughout the ages, people have suffered the most unspeakable hours and conditions in their workplace, rather than die or see family starve. It is the force of these powerful repressed instincts that drive us to seek security, that drive us to seek the highest possible

return on our investment, or that prompt us to sell perhaps at an unnecessary loss lest we be destitute. A human being needs security for
the future. On the material side, it is provided by currency to buy
goods and services, including health care.

The strongest of urges, therefore, can only be satisfied in the future, and they can only be satisfied with a promise of a monthly pension check and a promise of health care benefits in time of need. The
ultimate desire of each of us is to obtain a future with fundamental
needs (food, clothing, housing, health care) fulfilled. This is "security."
Each of us has heard that there is no "free lunch." Each of us is willing
to sacrifice now, to pay now for a guarantee of future security. The
need for future security, combined with the innate willingness to pay
now for a guarantee of that future security, makes us vulnerable to
schemes that take our present assets in return for a promised guarantee
of future well being. But schemes guarantee only an empty promise,
and time converts empty promises into bad dreams.

The promiser of dreams may not be a con man. He may be an
unwitting insurance salesperson or a well-intending broker. Witness the
hundreds of billions of dollars lost to investors of the Eighties in so-
called limited partnerships that promised tax relief and generous long-
term gains to those who would commit present and future years of
earnings. They collapsed because the basic economic scenario necessary
to make them work required better economic times than history has
ever provided. So it is said, the limited partners paid their money for
the deal maker's experience and the deal maker gave the limited partners an experience for their money. Or, the promise may have been
from an unwitting insurance salesperson for "Executive Life" selling the
investor an annuity or guaranteed investment contract to provide for
the meager years. He promised a return greater than any other company. How many investors looked before they bought? Did the salesperson realize his promise was backed by junk bonds? Did the elderly
folks and pension funds who bought this dream realize that once un-
wrapped, it became a nightmare?

The perfect scheme to defraud an individual would be one that
promised a bright future for which the investor must pay now. It would
be even more attractive if it promised a brighter future than could be
purchased anywhere else for the same price. It must be one where the
investor can hold the promise, but must wait many years for its fulfillment. It must be one where payment is due now but the investor cannot actually tell for some period the value or existence of the promised
return. What promise could make us more vulnerable to our present

earnings than that of adequate currency to spend in our old age? What promise could make us more vulnerable than the promise of care when we are sick and enfeebled?

Is there any defense against these scheme-makers and these scenarios of ultimate despair? Yes, there is. That defense is knowledge. Knowledge of the structure of the financial and health care arenas and familiarity with the rules by which games in these arenas are played. This book is not a "get rich quick book," but a compendium and guide to help thinking men and women understand the basics of investment and health care planning. It offers a wealth of information to help each of us obtain a secure future with currency enough to meet our needs and care for our ills. The purpose of this book is to provide knowledge—knowledge that can prevent the investment of our life's gold from purchasing a return of tin.

Audience for the Book

This book is written for two distinct but related audiences. First, it provides a comprehensive introduction to assist the American consumer in acquiring the requisite information for achieving financial security and grasping the complexities of health care systems in the United States. Second, it is designed to advance the knowledge of health care professionals (doctors, nurses, health administrators, and so on), educators, chief executive officers, personnel and employee benefits managers and specialists, accountants and chief financial officers, attorneys, and others seeking a better understanding of the many facets of health care planning, income planning, and the relevant delivery systems in the United States.

Overview of the Contents

Part I, Chapter 1, "The Financial Arena: Retirement and Health Care Planning" describes the monetary arena and connects income, risk, health care, taxes, budgeting and estate planning into a logical sequence of events. We highlight this part as essential knowledge if one is to develop a strategic plan that increases the probability for success.

Part II, "Pursuing Personal Security" contains three chapters. In the first chapter, we describe the issues of today's business and the individual, the time value of money and money value of time and the funding methods for income and health care programs.

In the second chapter, we present an overview of taxes as they relate to health care and retirement planning and emphasize the need to develop a personal strategy in approaching these areas of lasting concern.

The third chapter provides an overview of the health care delivery systems: Health Maintenance Organizations (HMOs), Medicare/Medicaid and Fee-for-Services.

Part III, "Retirement Systems in the United States" presents a close look at specific retirement delivery systems in the United States. This part contains four chapters (Chapters 5 through 8) in which we examine, in depth, qualified and nonqualified institutional income programs, individual income programs, taxation of lump-sum distributions and personal considerations in preparing for retirement. This part contains essential information for organizational and individual planners in their pursuit of workable strategies that will increase the probability for success in a changing environment.

Part IV, "Health Care Delivery Systems in the United States" contains seven chapters. The first four chapters (Chapters 9 through 12) examine the three health care delivery systems, their advantages and disadvantages, implications for risk and legislation pertinent to health care. Chapter 13 covers payment reform.

In Chapter 14, liability in medicine is examined in relation to its impact on access, quality and cost of health care in today's political, economic and social environment.

Chapter 15 suggests some solutions that need to be considered in getting a handle on health care in the United States. These solutions are divided into three timeframes: immediate-, intermediate- and long-term.

We conclude the book with a glossary of terms, references, and an index.

Part I

Part 1

Chapter 1

The Financial Arena: Retirement and Health Care Planning

"Before I retired, I had plenty of money but no time; now, I have all the time in the world—and no money." Does this statement sound familiar? It should. It has been made by thousands of retired people, many of whom are getting older and poorer. Inflation has taken its toll, but the common reason for this predicament is that retirees did not plan.

Political, economic, social, and cultural environments and attitudes are rapidly changing. Consider the following:

- Life expectancy is approaching 80 years. If we retire at age 65, we have a life expectancy of 15-20 years after retirement.
- Mandatory retirement has been defeated. Nevertheless, more than one-half of the labor force takes Social Security before reaching age 65. This is a clear statement of real attitudes about working "forever" and about the changing "work ethic" in the United States.

3

- Children don't expect to provide for parents. Government programs are expected to take care of their income and health care needs.
- Many individuals are worth more dead than they are alive. Their real property and hard assets have appreciated enormously, and these become taxable at death. What's left is redistributed; frequently taxed again; then spent by others.
- Taxes will continue to take their toll during retirement years.
- Because most Americans today can expect to retire earlier and live longer, they will need to use more assets for their own security during their longer lifetimes.
- A large percentage of the current population will be elderly 25 years from now. The children and grandchildren of these retirees will face an increased tax burden. Presently, three workers pay taxes to support one beneficiary. By the year 2020, two workers will pay taxes for one beneficiary. This ratio ignores the enormous welfare rolls.
- Today's retired person paid approximately $25,000 into the Social Security system. He or she will get that back in less than four years without considering health care cost provided by Medicare. Since 1941, when payments started, Social Security has been a good deal for most people retiring in the United States. This, however, won't be true for today's young worker, who will pay considerably more money into the system and get back proportionately less. This phenomenon is called **generation passing.**

The Government's Message

The **Tax Reform Act of 1986** (TRA) was not tax simplification nor was it tax reduction; it was tax complication and tax increases. This act makes it considerably harder for young persons to accumulate funds for retirement and health care needs. Government, at all levels, wants more taxes while people are working, and more in the form of surtax or reduced benefits after they reach the age of 65 or become eligible for Medicare.

The TRA of 1986 emphasized the need to start income replacement planning early. The message is this: We must be prepared to finance a big part of our own retirement income and health care needs or be satisfied with subsistence living. The increase in salary reduction (401 [k]) programs and cafeteria plans, which allow the individual to select the type and level of benefit coverage they want for themselves and their family, indicates an acknowledgment by many companies that the individual employee must participate in taking care of basic retirement, health care, disability, and life insurance. Furthermore, corporations are asking employees to pay more out-of-pocket for health care coverage by requiring greater employee contributions for (1) health care premiums, (2) deductibles, and (3) coinsurance.

The Individual's Concerns

Everyone is concerned about the long-term effect of inflation on their future security—or they should be. The only way we know to beat inflation is to have more money—or assets to convert to money. However, we are making a mistake if we count on wages to automatically keep raising our standard of living. Furthermore, what happens once we retire and no longer work?

Today, income adjusted for inflation and taxes isn't keeping pace with expenses. Our average salary increases are far behind increases in the cost of (1) health care, (2) home ownership, (3) purchase and maintenance of automobiles, (4) utilities of all kinds, and (5) government services at the federal, state, county, and city levels.

The great retirement lie is that retirement is something we don't have to worry about until we are in our 50s or 60s, and then our pension or Uncle Sam will take care of us. Many U.S. companies inadvertently send this message to their employees by calling their retirement planning programs "pre-retirement planning" and making only those employees who are age 50, age 55, or age 60 and over eligible to participate. The message being sent to employees who are not eligible to participate is that they need not worry about retirement until they reach the designated age. Nothing could be further from the truth. The planning for retirement commences when one first enters the labor force. In fact, few of us understand much about our company's pension plan or about Social Security and Medicare, and we are not concerned. Retirement is just too far away to care. Hence, corporate-sponsored educational programs could appropriately be called "Income Replacement and Health Care Planning" or Life Cycle Planning.

Challenge for the 1990s

One of the key challenges facing U.S. employers in the coming decade is to establish retirement and health care planning communication programs with employees. Communication programs should (1) inform and educate, (2) recognize the employee as uniquely valuable, (3) solicit the active participation of every employee, (4) be supported by all echelons of management, (5) have and form a common base, and (6) develop a common perception.

We spend a significant portion of our lives within the employer community. Whether the business entity is profit-making or nonprofit is not relevant to this discussion. Supposedly, the path is well known: We work, receive income, raise and educate our children, and retire with dignity and financial security. Right? Wrong! Many retired Americans today live in fear—fear of dwindling Social Security benefits, fear of inflation, fear of inadequate and expensive health care needs, fear of higher taxes, and fear of crime. The greatest fear of all is running out of money. To discover the true meaning of discrimination in America, be older than 65, not working, not dead—but dead broke. The solution is understanding "income replacement" and health care systems and clearly focusing on life cycle planning at a young age. Personal dignity during our retirement years is not guaranteed.

Historically, corporate America has taken the position that the monetary affairs of its employees are personal matters of no concern to management. Changing demographics, social legislation, and escalating employee benefit costs make such an attitude obsolete. Furthermore, employers have a moral responsibility to provide timely, understandable, and pertinent information, even if for no other reason than corporate survival.

We believe that there is no institution better equipped to assume the education function than the employer. This accountability is best satisfied through the establishment of a continuous and consistent information program sponsored by the employer. Employees respond to this type of decisive leadership.

This program should include information pertinent to estate planning, household budgeting, taxes, sources of income, social security, retirement plans, short- and long-term disability programs, group life insurance, and health care plans. The corporate program should integrate government programs, corporate programs, and the role of the individual in putting it all together. The employer-sponsored information program also should be open to spouses on a voluntary basis.

The Monetary Arena

The fundamental purpose of the monetary arena is to provide the foundation (common base) from which we can plan, develop, and maintain a common strategy to achieve short-, intermediate-, and long-term security needs. The United States has become a high-technology and highly legislated society dominated by confusion and distortion, not to mention personal invasion of privacy. We are saturated with bits and pieces of data from many sources. This infusion of information results from massive legislation passed by Congress. Anuually, Congress passes new legislation that impacts on estate planning, taxes, savings, earnings, retirement plans, health care systems, disability, and life insurance programs. There seems to be no framework to unite this data, no arena where it fits so a reasonable assessment can be made. This is particularly true if we perceive that someone else is paying for our income replacement, health care, disability, and death benefit needs.

It's not possible to successfully participate in any activity until we understand the purpose and rules of the arena. This is true of education, business, religion, war, or, our current interest, financial security, and health care planning. Today, we cannot rationally operate in the monetary arena unless we have acquired some knowledge about it.

Think of the monetary arena as a map. A map doesn't tell how to go from point A to point B. A map simply portrays where point A is located in relation to point B. Whether we go from point A to B via boat, air, car, or foot is up to us. Once we ascertain the mode of transportation (e.g., a boat), then we must select what type of boat and consider the logistical needs, cost, and time involved. Only we can and should make these decisions. Likewise, an effective income replacement and health care planning program addresses the alternatives in an informative and educational manner. We, as individuals, are responsible to execute and maintain these programs once they are decided upon.

Figure 1.1 shows a series of boxes, lines, a house, and dollar signs, and it is titled the "Monetary Arena." Consider this to be similar to diagramming a football field, a basketball court, a chess board, or a backgammon board. It really means nothing in terms of how the game is played; it simply diagrams the boundaries or the arena in which to operate or to develop a strategy. Figure 1.2 adds the word **Income** to the title. The need for income is a common denominator for all peoples of the world. Income is measured in money that is derived from labor, business, or property. An adequate amount and flow of income is

Figure 1.1 Monetary Arena

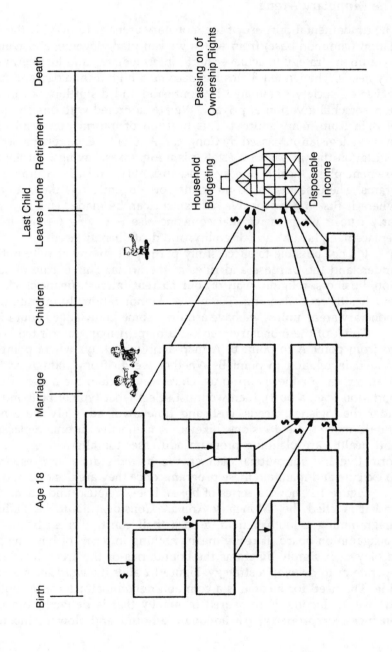

Figure 1.2   Monetary Arena—Income

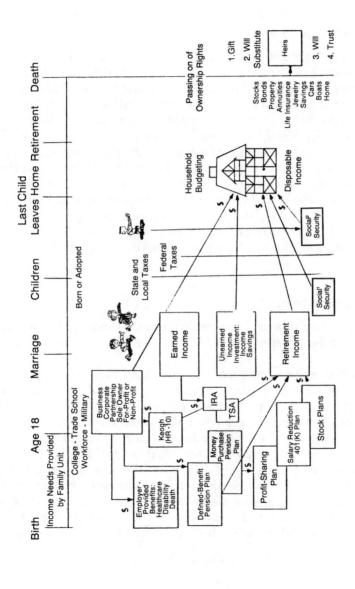

Birth   Age 18   Marriage   Children   Last Child Leaves Home   Retirement   Death

Income Needs Provided by Family Unit

College - Trade School
Workforce - Military

Born or Adopted

Employer-Provided Benefits:
Healthcare
Disability
Death

Business
Corporate
Partnership
Sole Owner
For-Profit or
Non-Profit

Keogh
(HR-10)

IRA

TSA

Defined-Benefit Pension Plan

Money Purchase Pension Plan

Profit-Sharing Plan

Salary Reduction 401 (K) Plan

Stock Plans

Earned Income

Unearned Income
Investment:
Income
Savings

Retirement Income

State and Local Taxes

Federal Taxes

Social¹ Security

Social² Security

Household Budgeting

Disposable Income

Passing on of Ownership Rights

1. Gift
2. Will Substitute

Heirs

3. Will
4. Trust

Stocks
Bonds
Property
Annuities
Life Insurance
Jewelry
Savings
Cars
Boats
Home

1. Subject to Income Tax
2. Tax-Free

essential to maintain and to provide for the necessities of life. The question is, "From where will we receive income as we progress through life?"

The Life Cycle Line

Moving along the life cycle line of Figures 1.1 and 1.2 from left to right, the individual marries and bears or adopts children; the children leave home, then the individual retires and ultimately dies. Of course, matters just aren't that simple. There are many variables that influence and cause substantial changes. Some people never marry or have children. There are wars, deaths of loved ones, illnesses, divorces, remarriages, job changes, career changes, continuing education requirements, and so forth. These changes are not necessarily good or bad, fair or unfair, just or unjust—they simply *are*. The sum of these experiences determines how we feel about any given subject. Everyone has different circumstances, needs, wants, and desires. Put another way, each of us is a uniquely valuable person in our own right, and our "uniqueness" comes with special needs that directly and indirectly affect our life cycle planning.

Sources of Income

There are three primary sources of income: (1) earned income; (2) unearned income (interest on savings or other assets); and (3) retirement income.

Earned income flows into our household from business as a return for labor or services. We may work for a profit-making or nonprofit organization, or a partnership or sole proprietorship. The key consideration is that we receive income as a return for our labor and services. Today, it's common for many households to have more than one income. This situation is commonly referred to as the "dual income" family.

Unearned income is not earned by labor, service, or skill. It flows into our household as a result of money deposited in a credit union, bank, mutual fund, money market fund, or savings and loan organization, or invested in stocks or other assets. This money earns interest or dividends or rental income, whether the recipient gets out of bed in the morning or not.

Retirement income flows when we stop working. Over and above Social Security benefits, retirement income may come from our employer's pension fund, a profit-sharing plan, a cash or deferred arrangement (401[k] plan), an individual retirement account (IRA), a tax-shelter annuity (TSA), a Keogh (HR-10) plan, a military or other government agency pension, a nonqualified deferred compensation plan (457), other source, or combination of the above. Since most contributions and earnings in these plans never have been taxed, these assets are subject to ordinary income tax as we receive them. By law, most income replacement programs require us to withdraw funds when we are no older than age 70 1/2. This is true whether we have retired or not.

Each of us need to keep our own records in our own files of all plans in which we've participated during our working careers. It is essential to leave nothing to chance and to depend on no one else to maintain these records. Otherwise, experience states, it won't work.

The very last item that we want to lose touch with is income. Income is what the entire planning process is all about. Each of us must have sufficient income to provide for the necessities of life—and to complete life on earth with dignity.

Taxes

Most of us overpay personal income taxes. Many people think that because an accountant completes their returns that they get all the deductions to which they are entitled; but no one can count on that. Accountants can only work with the figures provided by their clients. In the final analysis, it is up to each of us to make sure that we pay the government only what we owe. Be sure to keep detailed and accurate records as to your earnings and expenses.

Social Security taxes are calculated by the employer. A percentage of salary, as specified by law and matched by employers, is automatically deducted from pay. This payroll deduction continues until a maximum level is reached. (In 1992, that taxable wage base was $55,000 for Social Security and $130,200 for Medicare). Part of the money contributed in this manner is allocated to Medicare. Note in Figure 1.2 that Social Security is divided into two boxes. One box shows funds subject to income tax, and one reflects funds flowing into households free from income tax. Effective January 1, 1984, a single taxpayer with a modified adjusted gross income exceeding $25,000 or married taxpayers filing jointly with incomes above $32,000 must include up to one-half of their Social Security benefits as taxable gross income. Here is how it all works.

The Social Security taxes we pay and our employer pays each year are based on the tax rate and the amount of our taxable earnings. We do not pay Social Security taxes on earnings over the maximum taxable amount. This amount is $55,000 for Social Security and $130,200 for Medicare for 1992.

The maximum taxable amount increases each year, based on increases in the average wages and salaries of all workers in our country. The issue is that Social Security taxes have always increased, never decreased. In fact, many workers have taken salary reductions or no salary increases as a result of national economic conditions. Historically, these business cycles have been ignored by Congress.

There are two taxes that, when combined, are known as Social Security taxes. The two taxes are: (1) *Old-Age, Survivors,* and *Disability Insurance* (OASDI): This tax pays for income benefits to beneficiaries; and (2) *Hospital Insurance* (HI): This tax pays for hospital care for beneficiaries covered by Medicare. Let's look at two examples of how this works in Table 1.1. Suppose we earn $50,000. How much will we and our employer pay into the Social Security system:

Table 1.1 Employee and Employer Paid Social Security

	Tax Rate	Earnings	Tax
Employee (OASDI)	6.20%	$50,000	$3,100
Employee, Medicare	1.45%	$50,000	725
Total	7.65%		$3,825
Employer matches, dollar for dollar, what the employee pays			$3,825
Total Employee/Employer Pays			$7,650

$7,650 divided by 365 days equal $20.96, per day, each day of the year.

Suppose the spouse of this employee works and also earns $50,000 per year. When we combine the two employees and their employers, we find that they pay, in the aggregate, $15,300 ($7,650 + $7,650). $15,300 divided by 365 days equal $41.92, per day, each day of the year.

Suppose we earn $125,000. Table 1.2 shows how much we and our employer will pay on this amount.

Table 1.2 Employee and Employer Paid Social Security— $125,000

	Tax Rate	Taxable Amount	Tax
Employee (OASDI)	6.20%	$55,000	$3,410.00
Employee, Medicare	1.45%	125,000	1,812.50
Total			$5,222.50
Employer (OASDI)	6.20%	$55,000	$3,410.00
Employer, Medicare	1.45%	125,000	1,812.50
Total			$5,222.50
Combined Employee/Employer contributions			$10,445.00

$10,445.00 divided by 365 equal $28.62 per day, each day of the year.

Suppose the spouse of the employee works and also earns $125,000 per year. Combining the two employees and their employers, we find that they pay, in the aggregate $20,890. $20,890 divided by 365 days equal $57.23 per day, each day of the year.

These amounts represent Social Security taxes only. By the time we include federal, state, city, gasoline, property, sales, and the list of taxes and fees goes on and on—it has to make us wonder where all this is leading.

From the inception of collections for Social Security taxes in 1937 to 1949, working Americans paid a 1 percent tax on a maximum earnings of $3,000 or $30.00 per year. Employee and employer, combined, paid a grand total of $60.00 per year or 16 cents per day, each day of the year. This maximum of 16 cents per day is a far cry from the current maximum of $57.23 per day, each day of the year. This increase in Social Security taxes is astronomical even when one takes into consideration the toll inflation has taken from our purchasing power.

Personal taxes—such as income taxes, property taxes, and inheritance taxes—take a sizable chunk of income. What remains after taxes is disposable, discretionary, or spendable income; households are free to spend it as they see fit. For practical purposes, households divide their disposable income between "consumption" and "savings." In addition, a household might consume more than its current disposable income by drawing on past savings or by borrowing.

Budgeting

Budgeting is simply a tool to get what we want with our money. A budget coordinates "income" and "expenses." Generally, it guides us in planning, controlling, and recording expenditures. It's important to keep in touch with how we spent money in the past and how we are spending it now. Individuals who keep in touch with their spending and saving habits tend to have fewer financial problems, and this results in greater peace of mind, productivity, and personal well-being.

Budgeting helps us to learn where our money is going, to plan priorities, and to avoid falling deeply into debt without realizing it. Every month, thousands of charge accounts and credit cards are revoked or canceled, automobiles are repossessed, and home mortgages are foreclosed. More times than not, bad personal money management is to blame.

These are only three methods for financing current consumption: (1) we can take from our savings, (2) use present earnings, or (3) we can borrow against our expected future earnings. Like everything else in life, each of these methods has at least one potential pitfall. If we deplete savings by current spending, there will ultimately be nothing left for emergencies or income for the future. Spending current income prudently will eventually impact on our financial well-being. Pledging future expected earnings is the greatest sin of all and, unfortunately, the way that many Americans have maintained their standard of living in an inflationary environment. Federal, state, county, and city governments have been guilty of pledging future earnings for financing current consumption. Whether used by the individual or government, this method is courting disaster in the long term.

Budgeting is simply a method of providing knowledge about our finances. It is the individual's responsibility to use this information wisely and to benefit from it. Personal discipline and common sense are all that is required for successful budgeting.

Budgeting can help us get out of life what we want. A budget can be responsible for:

- Providing a tax record for the IRS.
- Assist in purchasing big ticket items.
- Minimizing interest and carrying charges.
- Enhancing family awareness and participation.

The last benefit may well be the most important reason to maintain a household budget. The number one problem causing families to end marriages is petty money squabbles.

Money

Three things can be done with money. You can spend it, rent it, or buy ownership into something. To spend it is an all too familiar concept. We simply pay money to buy goods and services. When we rent money, we simply go to a local bank, savings and loan, credit union, or money market mutual fund and make a deposit. In return, we receive interest on our money. The financial institution then finds a place to loan our money. When we rent our money to a financial institution, we are the legal owner of a claim against that institution. It's important, however, to realize that it is the control of the money—not the legal claim—that really counts. When we buy stocks, bonds, jewelry, property, or anything to which we take title, we are establishing an ownership or **equity position**. Over a period of time, the value of the purchase may appreciate or it may depreciate. The value of an asset beyond the total amount owed on it is the equity position.

We may ask ourselves, "What is money?" By itself, it is nothing. A philosopher might remind us that money is a symbol of energy. We can use this energy wisely or foolishly; generously or self-indulgently; freely, or greedily. An economist might say that money symbolizes labor, goods and services, or property. Some might say that it represents gold and silver. Whatever our view of money, it seems reasonable that it can seldom be received as a "gift." Money is borrowed or lent or invested. The receipt of money usually requires performance and an accounting of performance that is acceptable to the giver. George Bernard Shaw wrote, "The lack of money is the root of all evil."

Risk

There are certain risks involved with money. The key is to identify the risk and then make every effort to minimize each component. With regard to money, **risk** can be said to be the chance of financial loss attributable to uncertainty about the future. Components of risk include future business cycles, interest rates, liquidity, inflationary cycles, deflationary cycles, and the reaction time one has to respond to changes in the marketplace or market volatility.

Risk can be reduced through knowledge and diversification. Knowledge comes from our own experiences and from history. Diversification comes from selecting a variety of risk/reward investment vehicles.

Often, what happens is determined by what we want to happen. Therefore, we are not only a witness to our personal history, but also its agent and its author. Hence, it's essential that each of us have a clear picture of our need for income, and keep its relative position within the monetary arena in clear focus.

Death and Heirs

We need to be aware that the estate and gift tax arena is under close scrutiny by the government as it seeks new revenue sources to reduce the deficit or start a new spending program. The threat of higher taxes, and fewer ways to avoid those taxes, gives a new sense of urgency to how we pass on our accumulated assets to our heirs. Most attorneys, stockbrokers, and insurance agents call this process **estate planning**. Call it what we may, we must decide how we want our property to be disposed of upon our death and to declare our intentions in some manner. If no declaration is made, our property will pass according to state laws of succession.

We need to structure the provisions that distribute our assets so that they take into account all possible circumstances, including the possibility of untimely deaths of children or other named beneficiaries. We need to clearly focus on the different circumstances that might surface upon our death. Three major scenarios become possibilities for most families. First, what asset disposition should be made upon the death of one parent? Second, what asset disposition should be made after both parents die? And third, what disposition should be made of any property remaining after both parents and all children are deceased?

Updating of provisions will be necessary as circumstances change. As a minimum, revisions should be made when we marry or divorce, when children are born or adopted, when we move or start a new business, or when our general financial picture changes significantly.

Inflation, combined with the proliferation of employee benefit plans, have caused people to look more seriously at estate management, and trust in particular. Trusts create a relationship where one person, the trustee, is the owner of title to property, and is subject to obligations to keep and use the property for the benefit of another, called the beneficiary or beneficiaries. Trusts avoid probate and at the same time combine investment and possible tax-saving opportunities with the option to provide for the well-being of loved ones even after our death.

Planning how to distribute our assets, upon death, to our heirs may not be the most pleasant topic. However, planning does provide the opportunity to maximize what we pass along to our heirs. We are in an environment of escalating taxes, education expenses and long-term health care costs, and estate planning is certainly one of the best defenses to be sure our family is protected.

If no formal declaration is made when we die, our property will be dispensed according to state laws of succession. To avoid such disposition from being executed, we can select one or more of the following when distributing our assets:

- **Gifts**. The quickest way to reduce estate taxes and to avoid probate is to dispose of property before death, and the simplest way is to give it away. Current legislation permits each person an annual exclusion of $10,000 per donee.
- **Will**. A will is a written expression of our intentions about the specific distribution of our property. It is generally necessary to dispose of property that's not jointly owned and does not have a named beneficiary. If there is no will, the state will dispose of the property. Wills involve probate, which is costly and should be avoided.
- **Will Substitutes**. When we name a beneficiary on such plans as life insurance, pensions, profit sharing, individual retirement accounts, and property held in joint tenancy, the individuals so named will receive benefits when we die. Community property agreements provide that the covered property go directly to the deceased's spouse. Probate is avoided in these instances.
- **Trust**. Of all the estate-planning tools, the trust is one of the most useful, yet few people take advantage of it. Part of this reluctance is a lack of information or misconceptions about the nature and purpose of this arrangement. To rectify this, we can get information on "revocable living trusts" or "irrevocable trusts" from our local library. Remember, wills create probate, trusts avoid probate.

Employer-Provided Benefit Plans and Information

Two reasonable goals for employee benefit programs are to assist individuals in attaining their short-, intermediate-, and long-term security needs and to promote corporate human resources requirements. This implies that there is an agreement whereby the employer and employee work together in these matters, not as adversaries.

There are two primary sources of information on employee benefits: the employer and the local public library.

We should know and thoroughly understand all our benefits programs. Generally, the employer is concerned and interested in assisting us in meeting four basic needs as they occur: health care, retirement, disability, and death. We must know what options and needs we have as to additional or less coverage in any of these areas.

In addition, the local public library is a great source of information and reference material. Individuals should spend a minimum of two hours per month reading financial literature, connecting it to the monetary arena, and defining and refining it to fit personal strategy.

Employer-sponsored retirement and health care plans are a major source of income replacement and health care during retirement years when earned income stops. Employer contributions are generally tax deductible and interest earnings are allowed to accumulate on a tax-deferred basis. Income from a retirement plan becomes taxable only upon receipt. At retirement we will be presumably in a lower-income tax bracket than during our working years. Employer-provided health care plans are deductible to the employer and nontaxable to the employee.

An Unchanging Arena

The options and programs that connect within the monetary arena change. The monetary arena itself does not change. We may understand how a program works, but to be complete, our knowledge must include where it fits into the scheme of the monetary arena. Understanding where programs fit in the overall arena enables us to recognize opportunities and to expose the obstacles that lie in our way. Having a sound understanding of the monetary arena drastically reduces these obstacles, because we can identify them before they do serious harm to short-, intermediate-, and long-term financial goals and to security needs.

Changes in legislation do not alter the basic working principles of the monetary arena. What does change, however, are the specific programs that connect within the arena. For example, when the shot clock was introduced into professional basketball, the basic principles of the game did not change—only the techniques used for play execution. Remove the shot clock from the rules, and the game of basketball remains with its basic principles intact. This concept also applies to the monetary arena. The basic principles remain—only the techniques used in accomplishing various security needs change.

Summary

We are all operating within this monetary arena whether we know it or not. Therefore, we must understand how employer-provided benefits programs work; how to maintain a household budget; how federal, state, and local taxes and regulations apply to us; how social systems fit into the scheme of things; how income replacement plans work; how to provide for health care needs; how to transfer ownership rights to heirs; and how to provide for income to live with dignity.

Part II

Chapter 2

Pursuing Personal Security: Grasping the Issues

Business and the Individual

Businesses are an integral part of the entire social, economic, cultural, political, and physical environment of our communities. As a social institution, business exists within the larger framework of society. Its continued existence depends on how well it fulfills its responsibilities as society perceives them.

The American economy has grown more complex. We who must work and live in this involved world of business must understand various disciplines underlying our decision making, which stresses analysis over rote learning. Like leadership, business is an art—an art of combining labor, national resources, and capital in a process that leads to the sales of goods and/or services. Business administration consists of policy formation, management, and the direction and control of scarce resources.

Effective business administration consists of knowledge in accounting, finance, human resource management, insurance, risk management, real estate, land use, communications, business plans, money and banking, decision making, the legal environment of management, economics, and statistics. International business is rapidly becoming an arena that can no longer be ignored. Business administration functions within the framework of business, the institution.

To develop an acceptable level of trust, other factors must be maintained by the organization. Organizational health, like personal health, is nearly impossible to maintain unless there is open communication, teamwork, and an effective handling of conflicts as they occur. This is especially true today, where we find our national manufacturing base in a state of neglect. No quick fixes will do the job.

Add "downsizing" to the difficulty in developing and maintaining an acceptable level of organizational trust. "Downsizing," the need for running "mean and lean" and "getting rid of the deadwood" to achieve a competitive edge, can lower morale, lessen commitment, and raise employee stress and anxiety. Downsizing can also leave the organization inefficient in maintaining a high quality of service to the customer. For example, demand for service exceeds the capacity of the corporation as a result of laying off personnel.

Executive pay has also added to the difficulty in developing and maintaining an acceptable level of trust. Each year brings reports of executive pay for the preceding year. *Business Week* informs us of the incredible annual salaries paid to corporate executives. $2 million to $60 million for chief executive annual pay is not unusual. These salaries do nothing to enhance an acceptable level of trust within the corporate entity. The salary spread between senior executives and "other corporate employees" is only part of the divisive policies operating in today's business environment. Consider the gap in income replacement or pension funds available to senior executives and the rank-and-file employee. It's true that qualified retirement plans, by law, cannot discriminate, but discrimination is the order of the day when it comes to nonqualified deferred compensation retirement plans. Such programs place an enormous burden on future corporate earnings. We are all familiar with polls listing the "ten best dressed men and women in the world" and the "ten worst dressed men and women in the world." Now we find ratings listing the chief executive officer (CEO) who had provided shareholders the "least for his/her pay for the year." That such a poll even exists tells us that something is drastically wrong at the top.

Realistically, senior executives should probably not receive a corporate retirement—period. If a person making millions of dollars each year is unable to provide for their future security, then how can they possibly be competent to provide the leadership necessary for the corporation to survive in the long term?

Today, corporate executives are not sharing the pain of the non-highly compensated employee, just as members of Congress are not sharing the pain of the very people they are representing. Congress votes to increase taxes, then votes to increase their own compensation package. After years of such behavior, the members of Congress wonder why they "get no respect." Senior executives find themselves in the same, "I get no respect" box as politicians. In viewing the entire arena, why would this response surprise anyone?

Having made these comments, let's view each of the categories necessary to develop and maintain an acceptable level of trust by the organization—any organization.

Developing an Acceptable Level of Trust

Trust tends to be like a combination of weather and motherhood: weather is widely talked about and motherhood is generally assumed to be good. Presumably, trust means that members of organizations can rely on the integrity of what others may say and do. Where there is trust, there is the feeling that others will not take advantage of us. It means energies do not need to be diverted from productive tasks to acts of self-defense. Blame tends to be de-emphasized and problems, rather than people, are attacked. Building an acceptable level of trust is probably one of the most difficult goals to achieve in business development. Not everyone can share equally in the fate of the group. Those within the group are generally more concerned than those outside of it. Stress from external factors on group members can prevent them from finding the time to devote to the development of genuinely trusting relationships.

Nevertheless, many organizational changes and development efforts can likely increase or improve very low levels of trust up to some moderate or at least acceptable levels. No matter how well-grounded one may be relative to the business arena, it is crucial that organizations attempt to develop at least a moderate level of trust, because trust appears to be necessary if an organization is to prosper and remain functional.

Open Communication

This involves the implementation of accurate information: one party providing facts to another party, regardless of the facts. It is the willingness of individuals to say what they mean. Even with the existence of trust, it is not easy for employees to develop the habit of open communication. We learn to be open; and like any other learning, the process may be slow and at times painful.

Handling Conflict

When trust and openness of communication are absent or not at an adequate level, the organization will not be able to bring conflict into the open. We can't deal with conflict if we are denying its existence. Since conflicts **will** occur in any organization, the problem is to prevent the organization's denial so that contention can be faced and resolved rather than be allowed to threaten the performance of individuals and the total system.

Handling conflicts is time-consuming in the short term, but time-conserving over the long term. It permits individuals to disagree, but it also permits individuals to work out their differences with an elevated understanding and respect for one another.

Teamwork

Teamwork is based on the supposition that limited resources, time, money, material, and people can be shared among the participants in a cooperative manner, and that it is possible to increase the quality of the resources themselves.

As our business environment becomes more highly specialized and complex, success depends more and more on the effective interaction of individuals and groups. Each business must evaluate to what extent teamwork is necessary and desirable. Like most factors, diminishing return sets in at some point.

Keeping the Organization Well

Unless business is able to develop this capacity, the accomplishment of the other factors will not count for much. Keeping the organization "well" is in everyone's interest.

We emphasize organizational health because of the pressures put on business by the ever-changing and increasingly dynamic environments in which it operates. Organizational health is essential to prevent the inevitable decay that will occur without it. Both the individual and business need to:

1. Learn from experience.
2. Learn how to learn; to improve the learning process.
3. Get in touch with our future.
4. Learn how to plan.
5. Learn to manage our individual and business affairs, especially during turbulent times.
6. Be responsible for our own destiny.

The problem for business revolves around not whether it wants to develop along these lines, but rather how to do it.

These statements are the cornerstones or the foundations in which business operates. Implementation of these concepts is useless unless one has a grasp of how they interact. Success is contingent upon human input, interaction, interdependency, and execution.

Today, we are vitally interested in the practices that govern the conduct of business in providing goods and services to consumers. The real humanities of our times are found in the study and application of business. American business today is a direct reflection of our political, economic, cultural, and social philosophy. Good or bad.

During the past 100 years, the evolution of business has been a general process of economic growth that has produced ever larger business units. The changes in economic and social institutions, such as the growth of labor unions and the increased importance of government at all levels, have presented to business a whole new set of problems. Furthermore, the methods used by business in attacking the problems of trade, of price competition, and of weak financial policy have had a significant impact on profits. These methods are leading to the ultimate conversion of the American business community to the so-called high technology, information, and service economy. This has been detrimental to our manufacturing base.

Business will be challenged during the coming decades to find solutions to problems that form a social, economic, political, and cultural base. The business environment will dictate the need for analytical minds with vision and imagination. Without individuals, there is no business.

Time Value of Money

The only way to combat inflation is to have more money or assets to convert to money. If we are counting on wages to automatically keep raising our standard of living, we need to think again. Besides, what happens once earned income stops, when we retire and no longer work?

A temporary stop-gap to salvage our standard of living has been the increase in the number of dual-income families. This is only a stop-gap, and within a decade it will be inadequate to sustain our current standard of living. Inflation and health care costs, combined with taxes, low productivity, changing demographics, drug abuse, weakening of the work ethic, and litigation, are just a few of the factors that are weakening the vitality of our country.

Given our environment, we cannot start thinking about retirement a year or two before the gold watch presentation. It's simply too late. Even if we start ten years before retirement to acquire the capital necessary to provide for our security, we still will only have a minimum amount of time to get the job done. Ideally, people should start acquiring that money while they are still in their prime working years. We need to pay ourselves first. Stop working for everyone except ourselves and our family. Money and hard assets will always get us through the turbulent times that are sure to occur during our lives. We will have money only if we pay ourselves first and understand the concept of "time value of money." All financial institutions in America understand and practice time value of money.

Time value of money is the opportunity cost of money. If we tie up our money in a particular use, the opportunity cost is the earning power the money would have had if we had used it in other ways.

For example, assume we were offered an opportunity to invest $1,000 today with a payoff of $1,080 in two years. If, instead, we put that $1,000 in a savings account at our local bank to earn interest over the two years, the $1,000 we have in our hand today could be increased to a future value greater than $1,080. This is because money, at any given time, can be converted to an equivalent greater value at a later date by calculations called **compounding**.

Here's how compounding works. Suppose our savings account could earn 5 percent interest, compounded annually. This means that each year our $1,000 deposit is increased by a factor of .05. At the end of one year, we would have $1,050; at the end of the second year, we would have $1,102.50. Obviously, our offer for a payoff of $1,080 two years from now through the investment opportunity mentioned above is not as much as the savings account alternatives. That's the opportunity cost.

This example demonstrates the three factors at work in determining the time value of money:

- How much money do you have?
- How much time can it work?
- How much can it earn?

The constant interaction of these three variables—time, money, and earnings—will determine how much money we will have in any given time frame.

The time value of money is also at work in qualified retirement plans. And since our contributions are generally tax deductible, our earnings are allowed to accumulate on a tax-deferred basis. This means that we are able to keep money in our investment account that would have gone to local, state, and federal taxes. This is why elective contributions to qualified deferred compensation programs are an essential part of providing for our long-term security needs. If our employer offers such a program—enroll. If we are eligible for a tax deduction by contributing to an individual retirement account (IRA) under current regulations, participate.

Table 2.1 shows what a one-time investment of $10,000 would be worth at the end of various time frames and interest rates. **Table 2.2** shows how much an ongoing monthly contribution of $100 would be worth at the end of various time frames and interest rates. The younger we start "paying ourselves first" under favorable tax circumstances, the more we will have to provide for our long-term security needs. Get started now—it's never too soon or too late. Our employer can help us get started.

Money Value of Time

Suppose we can spend our time either repairing cars at $60.00 per hour or choosing stocks for our investments, and we are quite good at both. The opportunity cost of repairing cars represents the profits that we could have earned buying and selling stocks; the opportunity cost of buying and selling stocks is the money we could have earned repairing cars.

Let's suppose that we spend four hours per month handling our investments, which results in a return for the month of $100, which is $25 per hour. If we turn our investments over to a professional manager who could generate $75 per month, net of fees, then the opportunity cost of spending time repairing cars, rather than managing our money, is $100 minus $75, or $25. Since $25 in investment profits is sacrificed to four additional hours for repairing cars, the hourly opportunity cost is $25 divided by four, or $6.25.

Since we can earn $60 per hour repairing cars, our comparative advantage is now clear. Hourly earnings from repairing cars, net of opportunity cost, are $60 minus $6.25, or $53.75. Even though we can earn more than the professional investment manager, we are better off concentrating on repairing cars.

Table 2.1 Comparative Interest Growth Chart

In Five Years $10,000 Will Grow to...

Interest Rate	Future Value
7.00%	$14,025.00
8.00%	$14,693.00
10.00%	$16,105.10
12.00%	$17,623.42
14.00%	$19,254.15
16.00%	$21,003.42

In Ten Years $10,000 Will Grow to...

Interest Rate	Future Value
7.00%	$19,671.00
8.00%	$21,589.00
10.00%	$25,937.00
12.00%	$31,058.00
14.00%	$37,072.00
16.00%	$44,114.00

In Twenty Years $10,000 Will Grow to...

Interest Rate	Future Value
7.00%	$ 38,696.00
8.00%	$ 46,609.00
10.00%	$ 67,275.00
12.00%	$ 96,462.93
14.00%	$137.434.90
16.00%	$194,607.59

Table 2.2

In Five Years $100 of Monthly Contribution Will Grow to...

Interest Rate	Future Value
7.00%	$7,159.20
8.00%	$7,346.70
10.00%	$7,743.70
12.00%	$8,166.90

In Ten Years $100 of Monthly Contribution Will Grow to...

Interest Rate	Future Value
7.00%	$17,308.40
8.00%	$18,294.60
10.00%	$20,484.40
12.00%	$23,003.80

In Twenty Years $100 of Monthly Contribution Will Grow to...

Interest Rate	Future Value
7.00%	$52,092.60
8.00%	$58,902.00
10.00%	$75,936.80
12.00%	$98,925.50

Taking Care of Basics

The basics for which we must all provide are health care, retirement, disability, and death. Of these basics, only health care requires continuous attention from **birth** to **death**.

The Players

The **basics** are provided by the following **players**:

- Mandatory government programs such as Social Security, Medicare, Medicaid, unemployment insurance, workmen's compensation, and disability income. We and our employer pay for these programs. Governmental agencies collect our taxes, redistribute the money, and administer the following statutory programs.

- Employer and union provided benefits
- Our personal savings and voluntary insurance programs which might include additional coverage for health care.

In the process of taking care of **basics**, whether it's government, our employer, our union, or ourselves, there are only three funding methods:

1. Pay-as-you-go
2. Terminal funding
3. Advance funding

It is **essential** that we understand how each of these funding methods work. We must understand each of these funding methods in order to understand the probability for achieving our short, intermediate-, and long-term security needs.

Pay-As-You-Go

Contrary to what many believe, in the long term any program that professes to take care of the basics by using this payment method is really taking care of little. Why? Because the benefit program promised is not an insurance plan based on our contributing money that is invested until our time of need (actuarial funding).

Then, what kind of program is it? A **pay-as-you-go system** is one in which taxes are collected from us, our employer, or both. They are not invested for our future health care needs. These funds are immediately paid out as benefits to those who are currently "eligible" to receive them. The most common pay-as-you-go program, and by far the **biggest** in America, is our National Social Security Program. Social Security provides for our Old Age, Medicare, and Disability. On January 1, 1988, our government, for the first time, collected over 15 percent from us in the form of a payroll tax.

During our working years, we and our employer pay a substantial sum of money into this system. The younger we are today, the greater the probability that when our time comes that we will collect only a small portion of the health care benefit for which we and our employer have paid. Why? Because our funds are now being used to pay health care benefits to current retirees whose benefits far exceed what they've paid into the system. As our retirement community expands (and it will), and the labor force shrinks as a percentage of the total population (and it will), some future generations will not get back the income and health care benefits for which they have paid.

If one is 40 years old or younger today, the probability is that he or she will not receive, dollar for dollar, what they've paid into the system. (**Forget** the enormous benefit of time value of money and **forget** what inflation will have done to the purchasing power of those dollars that they have paid.)

The risk in using the pay-as-you-go method of funding is that the government will be unable to collect sufficient money to provide the benefits to us when we and our employer were paying an ever increasing amount of money into the system.

During the early years of a pay-as-you-go income and health care program, there is seldom a problem. However, look what has happened in the United States to present future generations with an enormous problem:

1. The population has aged in both numbers and as a percentage of the total population. This unprecedented increase in the number of elderly and retired people is placing great pressure on income and health care cost.
2. Accumulation of interest on invested funds (time value of money) has been ignored in the basic design of our existing pay-as-you-go funded Medicare and old age income benefit.
3. The government is dependent on a constricting labor force to pay current taxes at a level necessary to support this increasing elderly population.
4. Prices in providing health care have risen faster than general inflation.

Each of these factors bring pressure for program reform; considered jointly, they *demand* program reform.

Terminal Funding

Through the **terminal funding** method of our health care or income replacement program, we or our employer (or both) set no money aside until we are confronted with a need. At that precise moment, we or our employer (or both) reach into our pocket, and from current cash flow, come up with the singular sum of money necessary to pay for a particular illness.

When we need benefits, terminal funding creates an uncertainty within the political, economic, and social environment. Who will guarantee that a sufficient sum of money will be available under current cash flow requirements? There is a danger or risk in using this method because the funds may not be there when we need them to pay for our care. Our cash flow availability might be inadequate.

Advance Funding

The **advance funding method** anticipates and clearly recognizes that we are all at substantial risk relative to income replacement and health care. Accordingly, these programs are designed, implemented, and paid for by using sound insurance and actuarial principles. Assets are deposited into trust accounts and can only be used for those purposes for which the accounts were established. Advance funding gives us the greatest probability for success in achieving our short-term, intermediate, and long-term security requirements.

We live in an ever-changing environment that exerts political, economic, and social pressures. Through advance funding, fine tuning is made annually (sometimes more frequently) to accommodate actuarial adjustments necessary as a result of governmental legislation, inflation, or other economic or noneconomic factors.

Time value of money is the foundation of advance funding. When the need is there, the money is there to provide the promised benefit. Sound insurance and actuarial principles are applied in getting the job done.

In the long term, advance funding offers the greatest potential for providing adequate health care needs. We must recognize that no government and no employer in any society can guarantee or protect us from every risk. This is true of any plan or funding method used in the short, intermediate, or long term.

Clearly, health care and income replacement are commonly used and needed by most of us during our lifetime. Health care must be paid for. The question is: Which method or methods of funding should our nation use?

Financial Realities

The United States government overspends its revenue receipts by huge amounts. The roller-coaster movement of the dollar on international exchange markets shows that investors, both in America and abroad, have lost confidence in the soundness of the American economy.

Currently, there are a number of immediate problems facing our nation. Consider:

- The savings and loan situation—the bill increases each day
- Third World debtors
- Federal deficit
- State, county, and city deficits
- Continuing business decline after an elongated seven and one-half year cyclical rise
- A host of welfare expenditures and new proposals for redistributing income and wealth
- Consumer debt
- The situation with insurance companies
- Banking problems—much of which is tied to the Third World debtors
- Possible refusal of foreign investors to continue financing our snowballing debt

All of these events are playing a major role in making the United States the world's largest debtor nation.

If we fully institute an unfunded national health care program, coupled with the aforementioned problems, we will prove to foreign investors that we have no intention of changing our irresponsible and spendthrift habits. The end result will probably be a system of socialized medicine that will impose tough rationing and will deny health care to millions of Americans. We'll be fine as long as we only have a common cold. But, whatever we do, don't get old and become seriously ill. If we do become seriously ill and are not wealthy, we will quickly discover the concept called the "rationing of health care." Furthermore, we will also discover, painfully, the "means test." The "means test" is that if we have worked hard, have been responsible, have provided for our future, and have paid taxes, then social security income replacement and health care, as promised under Medicare, will be reduced significantly or taken away completely. We should not be shocked when the "means test" is passed by Congress because this type of thinking is prevalent.

Good Intentions

National health care probably is one of the best intentioned programs to benefit society at large. To mention that we are in favor of providing access, quality, and reasonably priced health care to all citizens is a commendable position. Who would dispute such a position? It's like saying we are: against **war**; for **freedom**; against illegal use of **drugs**; for **motherhood**; against **crime**; for **quality** education; against **homelessness**; for a **clean** environment; and against **poverty**. The list goes on and on. It sounds like a political platform for every politician in office and those seeking office. We all know the line well. We Americans love the fantasy world of good intentions, which often is an escape from reality.

Bad Result

Substantial socialization of medicine already has taken place. The present system of political entitlement points toward a bureaucratic structure of semi-socialized medicine. Promised entitlement programs payable to beneficiaries greatly exceed our ability, as a taxpayer, to pay, thus causing budget deficits. This is not a recent development. It has taken us 50 years to get to our national, corporate, and personal budget deficits. This scheme of political mumbo-jumbo consumes income and wealth and builds pyramids of enormous government debt that, in turn, amount to a tax lien against future income taken from future generations. Furthermore, such policies provide an open invitation to inflate our currency. Keep in mind that inflation flushes away debt at the expense of money-holders and savers. Inflation can create a society of speculators, where despair and restructuring of a society is the end result.

We must understand how institutions function in America:

- The monetary arena
- Retirement delivery systems
- Health care delivery systems and
- Provide for death and disability

The manner in which we have dealt with taking care of the basics during the past 50 years **has not worked**. We have transferred our personal responsibilities to government and business, and they have been too anxious to take the task in hand. In short, government and business have displayed a paternalistic attitude toward their citizens and employees, and we've never been the same. We now live in a fantasy world of make believe, where we look outside of ourselves for answers, although the answers have always been within us. Today, many government programs are insolvent, and business needs our help.

Now, everyone wants to sell us a horse to pull our cart. But first, we need to discover the cart; that is, the delivery system that will provide us and our family with our short-, intermediate-, and long-term security needs.

Acceptance of personal responsibility, in all of its facets, constitutes maturity. Maturity is viewing life as neither good nor bad, fair nor unfair, just nor unjust. Life simply *is*. It's what we, as individuals, do with life that matters; what we do for humanity today; what foundations we lay for future generations; what support we provide by pooling our individual strengths. Furthermore, maturity is the recognition that we can provide for the dignity and well-being of our families only to the extent that we are able to perceive and actualize ourselves in the physical environment as vital, knowledgeable, productive, and contributing persons.

Our physical environment certainly has political, economic, social, and cultural implications. And at some point in time, the mundane aspect of these implications—the monetary arena—causes difficulty between what we *need* and what we *want*. This arises in all areas of our life in matters concerning pleasure, money, wealth, and comfort. The desire for recreation and pleasure is basic, and the need for money and sufficient wealth to maintain a reasonable standard of living is not in dispute. However, the appetite has a way of growing. For instance, the vacations that we think we need become longer and more frequent; the social life becomes more demanding, and the time and money spent on the pursuit of pleasure becomes increasingly more extensive.

Today, it seems impossible not to be concerned about all aspects of our physical environment, including economics and the monetary arena. But these matters become easier to deal with when we realize that everything we possess is a gift; that we only have the use of these goods during life; that we need to invest back to humanity; and that we can't give what we don't have. When we as a nation have faith and love, and are willing to sacrifice in order to serve humanity, then peace of mind will be easy. The use of money is a daily moral issue that requires attention, management, and knowledge. It also requires that old standby—wisdom.

As a society, we must not forget that money is a positive energy only to the extent that wisdom is the basis of the knowledge for its acquisition and use. If there is negative energy resulting from a lack of ethics in either the knowledge or acquisition behind money—if wisdom is not present—then we can and do create more problems than we can handle as individuals and perhaps as a nation. We can't give something that we don't have because we have lost it to self-indulgence. Furthermore, we can't apply wisdom to knowledge when we haven't first acquired the knowledge.

If we apply ourselves to acquiring knowledge and keep our intentions and efforts ethical, more is shown and given to us each day in a perceptual manner. Herein lies the excitement and promise of being: of feeling a part of time, family, community, and society.

Part of the process in understanding the issues is to be sensitive to the political, economic, and social environments in which each generation is destined to live and what each generation passes to the next generation. The book *Generations* by Strauss & Howe describes the G.I. generation as Americans born between 1901 to 1924, who total 63,000,000 with 29,000,000 still living. The G.I. generation has a profound impact on our current political, economic, social, and cultural environment. G.I., of course, stands for "government issue." This generation has given us seven presidents. The last is President Bush. This generation has had a strong relationship and correlation with the growth of government at the federal, state, county, and city level. Government has become their benefactor. In fact, government has replaced some of the responsibilities previously delegated to the family. The G.I. generation has been instrumental in pushing deficit-financed programs, such as generous pensions and medical care, into the future for tomorrow's generations. This is a legacy that will last. Tomorrow's generations now face salaries that do not keep pace with inflation, face taxes that continue to rise, and face a high social security tax that will mean little or nothing when they are ready for it. Our younger generations are burdened with debt with little left over for accumulating savings. Social passages that the G.I. generation took for granted, like getting married, buying a house, having children and educating them; and providing for emergency funds, their own health care, and income replacement needs at retirement are enormous problems for our youth. Furthermore, how will younger generations repay the debt (federal, state, and local) being left to them by the G.I. generation? Realizing that this situation could threaten their survival, changes may occur. "Welfare" America could move to "free enterprise" America. Recognizing the threat could result in shrinking the power, scope, and the high tax-take of government. The people residing in Eastern Europe and Russia have clearly discovered, after much suffering and despair, that a welfare state doesn't work. The welfare state looks appealing in the short term. However, in the long term, to future generations, it strips them of their personal dignity and replaces it with human despair. Is the answer education? The answer is "yes." The next question is whether the existing institutional framework can get the job done? Most people would agree that we've had poor results of technical education in America despite the huge increase in funds expended. So what is the answer to the problem? Probably, the answer lies in removing government—federal, state and local—from education and turning it over to the private sector.

Does the Younger Generation Owe the Older Generation?

The implementation of Social Security, combined with the increasing financial strength of the elderly, have reduced the financial pressure on children to support their parents. Other changes may have a long-term impact in altering the parent-child bond. Consider:

- The increasing number of single parents
- The complexity of family relationships resulting from a high divorce and remarriage rate
- Small families
- Dual income families in which both spouses work, which may reduce a sense of obligation to the older generation

Parents today tend to expect to make fewer sacrifices for their children than in the past. They feel justified in this by demanding less from their offspring in the form of future obligations than what their parents demanded from them. When federal long-term custodial care legislation arrives, it will provide additional fuel to support this thinking.

The aging of America is forcing the issue, with a rapidly increasing number of older citizens demanding more income replacement and health care in expensive high-technology hospitals and nursing homes.

As a nation, we are now at the dawn of the first four-generation society in the history of the world. This new era can be one of passing on a rich, living inheritance of love, dignity, and wisdom, or it can be the beginning of an era of human suffering and loneliness, especially for the oldest generation, who could be living in utter despair.

Health care's political, economic, social, and cultural implications for our nation are enormous. No issues for the aging are more perilous than the area of health care and social services. This debate will be heated.

Chapter 3

An Overview of Financial Factors

Tax Aspects of Income Replacement

In order to contribute pre-tax dollars to a retirement plan and to realize the tax-deferred buildup of earnings, we must comply with certain principles. These principles follow rules and regulations legislated by Congress, published by the Internal Revenue Service, and known as the Internal Revenue Code (IRC). The rules provide the framework in establishing tax-deferred statutory retirement plans. All retirement programs that are currently tax-deferred will be taxable to us or our beneficiary upon retirement, disability, or death.

Since Congress is permitting us to deduct our contributions and granting the tax-deferral on earnings, certain restrictions are placed on our funds. For example, withdrawal from our account prior to age 59 1/2 will cost us a 10 percent penalty, plus inclusion of the amount withdrawn as ordinary income. We must start withdrawing our funds by April 1st of the year following the year we attain age 70 1/2. These are just two of the most obvious limitations imposed. For specific restrictions, refer to the section of the Internal Revenue Code under which your retirement plan is established. The numerous retirement programs and their various IRC sections are indicated in parts of this book. We don't have to be a retirement plan expert to understand how our retirement programs can serve us.

If our retirement plan fits in the general category of the previous paragraphs, then our plan is said to be "qualified," which means that our plan is afforded special tax treatment through meeting the requirements of the IRC. These tax advantages commonly include the following:

- If our retirement plan is sponsored by a company, that company is allowed an immediate tax deduction for the amount contributed to the plan for a particular year.
- We, as a participant of the plan, pay no current income tax on amounts contributed by our company.
- Earnings of the plan are currently tax-exempt, permitting the tax-deferred accumulation of income on investments.
- Reduced tax rates may apply to lump-sum distributions.
- Income taxes on lump-sum distributions may be deferred by rolling over the dispersal to an **Individual Retirement Account** (IRA), a rollover account, or to another qualified retirement plan.

The basic difference between a qualified and nonqualified retirement plan is that qualified retirement plans are given favorable tax treatment through meeting special requirements of the IRC. There is no special tax treatment for nonqualified retirement plans.

There is another important factor to consider when looking at qualified retirement plans. Contributions made to our income replacement plan will ordinarily be taxed at lower rates than our current compensation, since these benefits are commonly paid after retirement, when presumably we will be in a lower tax bracket. Just to keep the record straight, should we be concerned about the enormous tax-bracket that we will endure during our retirement years? We can only remark: Everyone should be so lucky. All retired persons in America should have a tax problem! We can assure you that this is preferred to the alternative—no money to tax. It's all about perception.

Inflation for some Americans means a financial boom; for others it means a financial crisis. Which is it for you? As government deficits at all levels increase, wages and costs rise, and the amount of money in circulation increases. This tends to cause a fall in the value of money and a rise in prices. If you're retired and living on a fixed income, you may well be in trouble. The most prevalent fear facing retired people is the fear of running out of money. Standing beside this fear of running out of money is inflation and the ravages it can inflict on the purchasing power of our dollar. This is a very real concern.

We must get in touch with this reality regardless of our current age. No government or private sector corporation can possibly guarantee **all** members of society protection from **every** economic misfortune that might venture into our lives. There is not enough money in the till. We have to look within ourselves for the answers that are best for us. We should consciously take care of commonplace events that can and do occur in our lives: retirement, health care, disability, and death. Since 1932, a great number of us have turned to government or business for answers.

Government thought it could solve our social problems by simply getting bigger and taxing more. Business took a paternal approach in dealing with their employees since, after all, the peak of the industrial revolution was here in America. There was a market for whatever was produced, regardless of the quality. Just in case things slowed down, we threw in the Korean and Vietnam Wars to help sustain us economically. We are still paying for those wars.

Today, government is looking to the private sector to solve our basic needs, after having had an uneven 50-year run at it, while the private sector is starting to look toward the individual to get involved. That individual to get involved, of course, is us. The real issue is that in our society we are not taught how to provide for income replacement, retire, provide for our health care and disability needs, and die. It is time that we were taught how to deal with the various institutions and service providers operating in America.

In planning for our basic needs of income replacement—health care, disability, and death—there are specific delivery systems available. This book discusses those delivery systems designed for income replacement and health care needs.

Remember, we have an income replacement program if we are setting aside funds for our retirement. If you are putting a few dollars into your till, you are to be congratulated, and by all means continue to accumulate. We cannot ignore that our individual tax liability may change after we retire. For some retirees, taxable income drops substantially, while for other retirees there is no change in taxes or they find that their income and taxes actually increase. No one has a crystal ball depicting what Congress may do in the legislative arena that specifically targets the retiree. However, one needs only to recall the *Medicare*

Catastrophic Coverage Act of 1988, repealed in 1989, to provide an acid test as to their frame of mind. This legislation placed a tax on those Americans eligible, not receiving, Medicare coverage. Imposed was a surtax on the elderly. The amount of this surtax was based on the amount of the individual's federal income tax liability.

Future legislation may impose a surtax on retirees along with a "means test" in order to remain eligible to receive Social Security income replacement and Medicare. Future retirees, who have worked hard, have been successful, and have planned for their income replacement and health care needs will not be eligible for Social Security benefits, or will receive a reduced level of benefits as dictated by Congress. These individuals will have paid huge sums of money to the government for income replacement and health care only to be denied its benefits through some form of "means testing."

Many Americans are in favor of a "means test." Their reasoning is that those who have should share with those who have not. After all, when it's all said and done, we are not taking any of our worldly accumulations with us when we die. Then there are those Americans who say that if we pay substantial sums of money, as dictated by Congress, for specific benefits, then those benefits should be made available as promised. For Congress to provide less than the promised benefits is taking our hard earned money under false pretense. Some call this behavior and policies, very simply, grand theft. Arguably, there are some moral issues involved in governmental behavior and programs of this kind. If the private sector administered their income replacement and retiree health care plans like Congress, then the entire board of directors would be in jail.

We must become very sensitive to tax legislation adversely impacting income replacement and health care programs during our working and retired years. Not to do so can make the difference between living our lives with dignity or in despair. In general, government programs are not a good deal. At all levels, governments tend to ignore the basic laws of economics in dealing with the distribution of goods and services and in dealing with social issues. Time value of money is seldom part of the design for any government programs. Advance funding is unheard of and future generation's cost is of little consequence. It is important to remember that government, at any level, can do nothing for any of us until they first take it from someone else.

Tax Aspects of Health Plans

Health care expenses paid for by our employer, on our and our dependents' behalf, are excluded from taxable income (which is subject to federal, state, and Social Security taxes). This means the company for which we work is allowed to deduct health care payments as an expense item on the corporate profit and loss statement. The individual who receives the benefit, our dependent, fellow employees, or all three are not required to declare the corporate dollars spent for medical care as income.

Suppose our employer paid us $3,000 in cash and told us to go shop in the private sector and to buy our own health insurance. First, we would have to pay federal and state taxes on that money. Secondly, we and our employer would both have to pay Social Security taxes. It should be clear to us that there is a large financial advantage in obtaining health coverage through an employer, rather than obtaining it on your own.

So what is the issue? The issue is tax revenue; that is, tax revenue as viewed by Congress. The *Tax Reform Act of 1986* does not allow a tax deduction on our tax return until unreimbursed personal medical expenses exceed 7.5 percent of our **adjusted gross income** (AGI). This equates to $750 for every $10,000 of AGI. When our employer provides and pays for our health care directly, this is a huge bargain for us, since we are not required to meet the 7.5 percent exclusion on employer payments. Consider what would happen if Congress decided that:

- Employers could no longer deduct 100 percent of health care expenses that it pays for us; or
- We, as the beneficiaries of this generosity, were required to declare as personal earned income a specified percentage of health care expenses paid by our employer. Taxes would include federal, state, and Social Security.

Obviously, a substantial increase in taxes would result. We would have less money. Congress would have more revenue to spend; that is, more revenue to spend in the short term. However, it can be argued whether Congress would have more money to spend in the long term.

If you work for a nonprofit employer, the end result for you is still the same—you would have less disposable income.

Think over the above statements carefully. Do you suspect such changes in policy by Congress might impact:

- How we use health care in the future
- Our personal standard of living
- The level of salary paid to us by our employer
- Taxes we pay
- Prices we will pay for goods and services.

You can be assured that these topics are sitting on someone's table, and in all probability that someone is currently a member of Congress looking for revenue. That someone may be the representative for which you voted. There are big dollars to be found here.

We must be honest with ourselves—any benefit that is employer paid tends to keep us uninformed and insensitive to the cost of the benefit. Whether the benefit is health care, income replacement, disability, or group life insurance, we tend to be better informed when our hand goes into our own pockets for the money. Since existing tax laws encourage our employer to pay 100 percent or the majority of nontaxable statutory benefits (health care is a nontaxable statutory benefit), these end results should surprise no one.

It's reasonable and moral that we should assume an obligation for the intelligent utilization of our benefits and, therefore, should help pay the cost. Especially in the health care expense arena, 100 percent reimbursement should probably not be allowed. If we have an obligation for intelligent utilization, and if we are responsible for providing for a portion of our security needs, then we should also have the opportunity to participate in the design of benefits. This concept in providing benefits takes us to flexible benefit programs under *Section 125* of the *Internal Revenue Code*. Are times changing? You bet!

What Are Cafeteria/Flexible Benefits Plans?

Cafeteria/flexible benefits plans allow us to choose our benefits. Not only can we choose our benefits, but we can also often select the level of coverage that we want within a benefit. Times are changing. For instance, consider that the labor force in the United States (a male primary wage earner supporting a wife and family) accounts for only a minority of households. In fact, if it is safe to say that there is no "typical" household, then it follows that "typical" benefit packages won't get the job done in providing for our basic security needs.

Also consider that the cost for benefits, especially health care, is a powerful driving force in moving us into the flexible benefits arena. When our employer offers us choices, then a clear distinction can be drawn between the level of benefits that we need and the cost for those benefits. We make the choice of adding benefits in place of salary, or reducing benefits and adding to our salary.

In order to contribute money into a cafeteria/flexible benefits plan and to deduct from our current income the amount of our contribution, we and our employer must comply with certain principles. These principles follow rules and regulations published by the Internal Revenue Service and known as the *Internal Revenue Code*. The rules that provide the framework in establishing a cafeteria/flexible plan must be a separate written plan that permits participating employees a choice between statutory nontaxable benefits and cash without having to pay taxes on the cash option unless they select it.

Many people loosely refer to all flexible benefit plans as **cafeteria plans**, but the term legally applies only to plans based on *Section 125* of the *Internal Revenue Code*. The plan must satisfy the nondiscrimination rules applicable to other welfare plans. Employers must provide the following information in the plan document:

- A description of each benefit offered
- Employer contributions that will be made on our behalf
- A salary reduction agreement between you and your employer
- Eligibility requirements to participate in the plan
- How we can contribute to the plan
- When and which of our benefit elections are irrevocable
- The window, or time frame, when we can enter the plan and for what periods our elections are effective

Under federal laws, some of our employer-provided benefits are considered taxable and others are considered nontaxable. State and local tax laws may or may not reflect these federal laws. A cafeteria plan may offer the following nontaxable benefits:

- Group term life insurance up to $50,000
- Accident and health insurance
- Some dependent-care expenses
- Disability benefits
- Some noninsured health expenses

In addition, the following taxable benefits may be included in a *Section 125* plan:

- Cash
- Group term life insurance over $50,000
- Dependent life insurance over $2,000
- Vacation

This list of taxable and nontaxable benefits does change. Check with your library, legal counsel, union officials, accountant, or your company benefits personnel for current information.

Flexible Spending Accounts

This portion of a cafeteria/flexible plan gives us a choice between taxable cash and pretax payment of nontaxable expenses. If this sounds confusing, read on. Under *Section 125*, our employer may offer a salary reduction option for medical and dependent care expenses, in separate written plan documents. If we choose to participate in a flexible spending account, we will realize the benefit of immediate tax relief, since deferred amounts are not subject to FICA (*Federal Insurance Contribution Act—Social Security*) and FUTA (*Federal Unemployment Tax Act*) taxes. This tax exclusion benefits not only us, but also our employer, since our employer is required to match our payment into FICA. Some of the expenses a flexible spending account can cover are:

- Health premiums
- Health/medical expenses not covered by the plan
- Health/medical deductibles
- Dental premiums
- Dental expenses not covered by the plan
- Dental deductibles
- Dependent care

Definition of a Dependent

The Internal Revenue Code defines any of the following as a dependent:

- Child
- Parent or ancestor

- Niece or nephew
- Aunt or uncle
- Son-in-law
- Daughter-in-law
- Father-in-law
- Mother-in-law
- Brother-in-law
- Sister-in-law
- Sibling, and
- Anyone living with you for whom you provide over one-half of their annual support

How Cafeteria/Flexible Benefits Help Control Costs

Flexible benefits is a delivery system or vehicle that enables us and our employer to clearly separate the level of benefits from the cost of benefits. Our employer can:

- Control options of benefits we can select
- Define benefit costs as a percentage of payroll
- Determine who will pay for increased costs
- Cap costs at a predetermined dollar level
- Increase or decrease benefits based on the level of productivity or profits
- Determine the price we will pay for the benefits

Some IRS Rules

When allowing our payroll deductions to be excluded from current taxation, the IRS imposes restrictions. For example, flexible spending accounts (FSAs) must meet all *Section 125* requirements; the most famous is the "use-it-or-lose-it" provision. This means that money left in the FSA at the end of the year cannot be carried forward into the next year or returned to us. Also, we must make our choices in a flex plan in advance of the plan (January 1-December 31), and no changes can be made in benefits or levels of contributions until the next period. However, there is an exception. Changes in choice are permitted for "family status" changes. A *family status change* is defined to include changes such as birth or adoption of a child, death of a spouse, divorce, marriage, legal separation, and spouse's termination of employment.

Flexible Benefits Recognize Us as a Uniquely Valuable Person

Flexible benefits plans start with one fundamental idea. They assume that we are different from all other workers—that we have unique wants and needs, and that these change during the course of our life and working years. From such a foundation, the attempt is then made, as far as possible, to offer us a variety of benefits from which we can choose. This process enables us to meet our many and varied types of family responsibilities and to tailor these programs based on our changing economic, family, and age cycles.

Getting a Handle on Retirement Plans—It's Never Too Early

Unless we have other income from savings and investments, a pension—combined with Social Security benefits—is likely to be our only source of income during retirement. If yours is a typical pension plan, it will promise to pay a certain amount each month at retirement, but only if you meet certain requirements. Often, these requirements are not understood, and we are disappointed to find that we may not have a right to receive the pension benefit that we had anticipated.

The actual pension plan that specified who gets a pension and how much monthly income that pension will provide is a legal document that is hard to understand. For this reason, companies are required by law to give us a summary of our plan. This summary is called a **Summary Plan Description** (SPD), and it describes in general terms our benefits and rights.

Today, it is not unusual for companies to set aside a percentage of their payroll toward a pension fund. Benefits are paid to workers who meet certain conditions. These conditions are usually determined by how long they work, whether they work continuously, and how much they earn.

The first question is whether we are covered by a pension plan. Remember, our company is **not** required to provide a retirement plan; that is, a retirement plan other than Social Security, to which they must match our contribution level. Approximately 40 percent of the private work force does not participate in pension plans. Even if they work for a company that has a plan, their job may not be covered or they may not be working enough hours to be included in the plan.

Once we are certain that we are participating in a plan, we then need to know what we must do to receive a pension at retirement. First, we need to know the number of hours our plan specifies that we must work before we are eligible to receive a pension benefit. After December 31, 1988, with a few exceptions, we cannot be required to work in excess of five years of service to be 100 percent vested under the Cliff Vesting Schedule; or in excess of three years for 20 percent vesting, with an additional 20 percent annual increase, thus providing us with 100 percent vesting after seven years of service with our employer.

Second, we must know which of our work years will actually be counted under the plan. If we take long periods away from our job, that time may be called a *break-in-service*. This can result in loss of credits for the years that we have worked before the break-in-service. Discover how your plan handles a break-in-service. Break-in-service will be discussed in your **Summary Plan Description** booklet provided by your employer.

Third, different plans have different ways of figuring whether we have earned a year of service. Usually, a year of service is credited to us if we worked a certain number of hours during that year. Generally, we will have a year of credited service if we have worked at least 1,000 hours during the previous consecutive 12-month period. The period starts with the date our employment commenced.

When we have worked sufficient time to have a legal right to a pension benefit, we have a "vested" right. Being vested does **not** mean that we can start receiving our pension. Being *vested* means that a pension benefit will be ours when we reach retirement age, even if we should leave the company.

Once we are sure that we will receive a pension at retirement, we need to know the amount of income that we will receive. The amount of our pension will normally be based on the number of years that we have participated in the retirement plan. After this is determined, we need to know how much income each year of credited service will provide. Remember, although our plan will normally accrue a benefit for every year of participation, we have no rights to that accrued benefit until we **vest** under the terms of our plan. At that time, we will have an accrued vested benefit.

The most common formula for figuring our level of retirement income is to multiply the years that we have been a participant of the plan times a percentage of our pay. Another method provides us with a flat dollar amount for each year that we have been a participant and covered by the plan.

For example, our retirement plan provides that we will receive 2 percent of our final average earnings. For our purposes, final average earnings is the highest five consecutive years in the last ten years of employment. If our final average earnings are $30,000 and we have worked ten years under the plan, our pension would be: 10 years times $30,000 times 2 percent equal $6,000/year or $500/month.

Under the **flat dollar formula**, our plan may give us $50 per month for each year that we have been covered by the plan. If we have worked ten years under the plan, our pension would be as follows: 10 years times $50 equal $500/month or $6,000/year.

Because our employer contributes matching money to Social Security, our plan may use a benefit formula that allows the company to subtract a portion of what they pay toward our Social Security benefit from our pension income. This is called **pension integration** with Social Security.

If we are married, we are required by the *Retirement Equity Act of 1984* (REA) to name our spouse as beneficiary under our qualified retirement plan. To avoid this requirement, we will be required to obtain a signed statement from our spouse declining or authorizing us to name someone else as beneficiary. This statement must be notarized or witnessed by our plan administrator. Furthermore, our retirement benefit may be reduced to provide a benefit for our spouse if we die first. This is called a **Joint and Survivor Annuity**.

We must analyze our own retirement plans. No one will do it for us. If you don't understand, don't hesitate to ask for help. Contact your Personnel Office/Employee Relations Department or the individual who administers your plan. You have the right to be fully informed about your pension plan. Your *Summary Plan Description* will tell you who to contact for information. If you have difficulty getting information, you should contact:

> Pension and Welfare Benefit Programs
> United States Department of Labor
> Washington, D.C. 20210

Anything that can have an adverse impact on our future security needs, especially sources of income replacement, should not be a surprise. We can avoid surprises by keeping ourselves informed. If your employer provides no informational seminars in this area of need, request that seminars be conducted.

In summary, here are some questions that we need to be answered:

1. Will I receive a pension? Find out how many years you must work before you can get pension benefits.
2. When can I retire? The age at which we can receive full pension benefits is called our **normal retirement age** (NRA). Often it is age 65, but this varies from plan to plan. Some plans provide for early retirement, usually at a reduced benefit.
3. Am I covered by a plan? If our company has a qualified retirement plan, we automatically become a participant in that plan at age 21 and after having worked a minimum of 1,000 hours during the previous 12-month period. If you are a union member, your pension is probably bargained in some manner. Check with your union officials.
4. How much of a benefit will I receive? Once I know I am covered by a retirement plan, I need to know the exact formula that will determine the size of my pension benefit. In most cases, my pension monthly income is based on the number of years that I have worked under the plan times a percentage of our final salary.
5. **Warning**: Many Summary Plan Descriptions include a statement that "if there is a difference between the information contained in this booklet and the legal pension plan and trust document, the plan document is the last word." If your SPD booklet contains this kind of statement, don't take it too seriously. The 11th Circuit Court of California ruled the opposite in 1985.

Survivor Benefits

All working Americans need to understand the *Retirement Equity Act of 1984* (REA), which was primarily created to provide pension equity for women and the nonemployee spouse under employer-sponsored plans. This legislation was **long** overdue.

If a participant retires under a corporate-sponsored retirement plan, the benefit is payable in the form of a **joint and survivor annuity** (J&S). If the participant dies before the annuity starting date, the benefit is payable to the surviving spouse. Prior to REA, the surviving spouse frequently lost all accumulated benefits, and seldom had any rights under the law. REA has changed all of that.

Here is what you need to know about REA:

1. A participant may waive the qualified joint and survivor annuity benefit and the preretirement survivor benefit **only** with the **spouse's written consent.** This waiver must be witnessed by a plan representative or a notary public.
2. Benefits payable under a qualified preretirement survivor annuity must commence no later than the month in which the participant would have reached the earliest retirement age under the plan (usually age 55), unless the surviving spouse elects to delay distribution further.
3. All qualified retirement plans **must** provide for an automatic survivor benefit. A stock bonus or profit-sharing plan may be **exempt** if: (a) the plan automatically distributes to the surviving spouse; and (b) the participant does not elect payment in the form of a life only annuity.
4. Before retirement benefits begin, the plan administrator must provide us with a written explanation of: (a) the terms and conditions of the joint and survivor annuity; (b) our right, as a participant, to waive the joint and survivor annuity; (c) the rights of the nonparticipant spouse; and (d) the right to revoke an election option, and the effect of a revocation.
5. Our plan is not required to provide the survivor benefit unless the participant and spouse have been married throughout the one-year period ending (a) the date the annuity payments begin, or (b) the date of the participant's death.
6. There **are** restrictions placed on immediate distributions from a qualified retirement plan. No immediate distribution can be made from any qualified plan, involuntarily, where the **present value** of the participant's vested benefit exceed $3,500. If the present value of the participant's account is **less** than $3,500, then an involuntary distribution may be made by the plan.
7. With respect to a participant loan, where the participant's vested plan interest is applied as security for repayment of such loan, the nonparticipant spousal approval is generally required.

If you, the nonemployee spouse, are asked to sign anything pertaining to your spouse's retirement benefits, be sure you know what you are signing. Answers can usually be obtained by contacting the employer.

The *Retirement Equity Act of 1984* provides the nonemployee with specific retirement benefit rights in the event of: death of a **vested** nonretired employee; immediate distributions from a qualified retirement plan; divorce; legal separation; and retirement payment options, to name only a few of the major areas that have long been of concern.

Your local library should have a copy of this act written in lay person's terms.

Annuities

When we are young, we tend to look to a life insurance company for protection against the risk of dying too soon. As we get older, we tend to become concerned about the risk of living too long without an adequate supply of money.

Annuity contracts were developed by the life insurance industry in response to this economic need. The economic need was for a guaranteed specified income for life after we reach a certain age or date. This insurance contract is aimed at solving the problem of living too long without financial security.

When used as an income-producing vehicle for retirement purposes, we should think of an annuity as being a lifetime periodic payment, normally paid each month, covering one or more lives. For tax purposes, our after-tax investment, if any, in the annuity contract is divided by the number of payments expected and that portion of each payment is nontaxable. The balance of our income, resulting from employer contributions, interest earnings on employer contributions, and interest earnings on our after-tax contributions is taxable as received. Your local IRS office will provide tables for computing the tax-free portion of your annuity income.

Nearly all defined benefit pension plans provide for lifetime incomes. At the time of retirement, it would not be unusual if our company bought a lifetime income for us from a major life insurance company. The cost for this benefit would be determined by: our age, the option selected for payout, the amount of monthly income that we will receive, our marital status, the cost of doing business on the part of the insurance company, the state insurance premium tax in our state, and other factors.

Types of Annuities

Some common types of annuity arrangements are:

1. Fixed Period Annuity: This is a contract that provides for periodic payments for a fixed period of time, such as 10 years or 20 years. This is **not** a lifetime contract.
2. **Single Life Annuity** (Also referred to as **Single Life Only**): A contract providing for periodic payments, usually monthly, for the rest of our life. When we die, the payments will stop. There is **no** beneficiary.
3. **Joint and Survivor Annuity:** This contract provides for periodic payments to us for our life and, upon our death, for the continuation of payments to a second person for his or her life. This option **must** be selected if we have been married for a period of one year prior to our retirement. To decline this option requires that our spouse sign a statement requesting the Joint and Survivor Option not be taken. This statement must be notarized. Annuities can be discussed as being either fixed or variable.

Fixed Annuity

Depending on the payout option we have selected, the amount of our first payment will remain the same for our lifetime under a fixed annuity. Risk has been transferred to the insurance company for mortality rate, future cost to the insurance company to do business, and earnings. The risk that we, the annuitant, assume under a fixed annuity contract is that inflation will cause our monthly income payment to be worth little or nothing as a result of the loss in purchasing power of the dollar.

Variable Annuity

Depending on the pay-out option that we have selected, the amount of our first payment will be fixed. After receipt of our first payment (normally lifetime monthly payments), each payment will vary based on the performance of the investment account. This is called a **variable annuity**. The insurance company continues to assume the risk factors for mortality and the cost of the insurance company to do business. We assume the loss or gain from the performance of the investment portfolio. The insurance company will normally charge us a management fee for handling investments, but we assume all risk for investment results. Check the prospectus for these costs and where your money is invested. No insurance company can market a variable annuity or an equity (stock) product without providing the buyer with a prospectus.

Inflation

A problem we all want to solve for retirement is the long-term effects of **inflation**—the loss of purchasing power of our dollar. Let's not kid ourselves—money is only worth what it will buy. No more, no less!

Having made that statement, let's look at the purchasing power of the dollar, today and in the future. From this day forward, the dollar can only pursue one of three courses relative to its purchasing power:

1. It will increase, or buy more.
2. It will stay flat, in which case the dollar will neither buy more or less.
3. It will decrease in purchasing power, or buy less.

When we purchase a fixed annuity, we are betting that either the first or second scenario will occur during our lifetime. However, if the third scenario occurs, and we enjoy a long life, then we may be in serious trouble; that is, unless we have other assets to absorb this loss of purchasing power.

Some individuals attempt to solve this dilemma by **split-funding**. This means that drawing part of their retirement income from the fixed, guaranteed annuity account, and drawing the balance from the variable annuity account. This split-funding may be 50 percent fixed, 50 percent variable, or any other combination, which is normally required to be in multiples of 10 percent.

Check with your annuity carrier to see your specific options. Study your options carefully before deciding. Remember, once you have selected an option, have signed on the dotted line, and have received and cashed your **first** check, you can **never** change. Therefore, this is a financial decision that will always be cast in concrete. Go slowly and make sure you thoroughly understand this income replacement delivery system.

For many Americans, the annuity is a lifesaver. For others, it could be a nightmare, since they lose control of their capital. Know what you need and know what you are getting. Understand your options and alternatives. Good decisions are a result of being exposed to timely and accurate information. Do your homework, and make the decision.

Do your own homework; then talk to an accountant, a tax attorney, and a pension specialist. Compare the results, then make your decision. A few dollars spent may save you a lifetime of grief.

Defined Benefit versus Defined Contribution Plans

Defined benefit and defined contribution plans can make a meaningful difference in how we will be living in the future. The following will provide an overview of the variety of retirement programs in the United States, and how they work:

Qualified Pension Plans

A **qualified retirement plan** is one of the best tax shelters available. Our employer is allowed a current tax deduction for its contributions to the plan. We pay no tax on money contributed for our benefit until a distribution is made. Furthermore, earnings from investments made with funds in the plan accumulate on a tax deferred basis, and distributions from the plan may be afforded favorable income tax treatment. Every working American should be covered and should be participating in a qualified retirement plan.

Defined Benefit Plans

A **defined benefit plan** provides a definitely determinable annual benefit. The level of benefit that we receive at retirement is clearly stated, with contributions to be determined. An actuary determines the required employer contribution each year, taking into account the level of benefit formula and certain economic and noneconomic factors. Among the most common of these factors are investment return, salary increases, and administrative expenses. Other factors include rates of death, turnover, and disability.

The most common types of defined benefit plans are fixed benefit plans, flat benefit plans, and unit benefit plans.

It is important to remember that our employer is already paying for a pension plan for us—Social Security. Social Security is a statutory requirement imposed on all employers and self-employed individuals in the United States. Taxes are calculated or rated for us and our employer. A percentage of our salary, as specified by law, **and matched by our employer,** is automatically deducted from our pay. This payroll deduction continues until we reach a changing maximum level of income. Keep in mind that part of the money contributed in this manner is allocated to Medicare. By integrating its retirement plans with Social Security, the employer gets the benefit of its Social Security tax payments.

If you have concluded that integrating the retirement plan with Social Security means a substantial savings to the employer, you are correct. In fact, the cost can be cut roughly by the amount the company pays in Social Security taxes. This tax is rapidly approaching 8 percent of your annual earnings with a $60,000 ceiling. We are not at these levels of contribution and income yet, but we'll get there soon. Integration with Social Security is commonly used in the United States by those companies maintaining a defined benefit retirement plan. This is true regardless of the benefit formula used to determine the final lifetime monthly income that we will receive from our retirement plan. Social Security integration laws are constantly changing, generally in favor of the employee, but we need to understand exactly how our pension plan works. Chapter 4 will talk about how to discover what your plan is holding for you.

A key feature that separates defined benefit plans from defined contribution plans is that under a defined benefit plan, a separate account is **not** established for each employee in the plan. The employer's contribution is placed in a general pool and actuarially allocated to past, present, and future service liabilities. Estimates are calculated by the plan's actuary.

In contrast, under a defined contribution plan, a separate account is established for all individuals who are covered in the plan. Actuarial work is neither necessary nor required.

Before going any further, let's review the term "qualified plan." A **qualified plan** means that the retirement plan is afforded special tax treatment for meeting a variety of requirements of the Internal Revenue Code. The principal federal tax advantages of qualified plans are:

- The plan is recognized as a tax-exempt statutory plan under a section of the Internal Revenue Code

- We, as a participant in the plan, are not currently taxed on the employer's contributions to the plan and are only taxed as we receive payments
- Our employer, if subject to tax, would receive a current deduction for amounts contributed to the plan. In a defined benefit plan, investment risk is retained by the corporation.

Defined Contribution Plans

A **defined contribution plan** provides for an individual account for each participant in the plan. Contributions, earnings and losses, and any forfeitures of accounts of other participants may be allocated to our individual account. Maximum additions to our individual account is the lesser of 25 percent or our annual earned income, or $30,000.

In a defined benefit plan, the level of benefit you receive at retirement is clearly stated, or fixed, with contributions to be determined. In a defined contribution plan, the level of contribution is fixed with benefits to be determined.

There are two types of qualified defined contribution plans: profit-sharing plans and money purchase pension plans. A stock bonus plan can either be a profit-sharing or a money purchase pension plan. In either case, the holder must be entitled to receive benefits in the form of employer stock. In a defined contribution plan, investment risk is transferred to the individual participant.

Whether participating in a defined benefit plan or a defined contribution plan, be aware that each type of plan favors employees who have certain characteristics. If we are young, in a lower pay scale, and will probably quit our job after a few years of service, then a defined contribution plan would generally be more advantageous to us. Why? Because a defined contribution plan usually vests more rapidly than a defined benefit plan; contributions are based on income, not on actuarial formulas: What we see is what we get. If we are 100 percent vested in our account, then the entire balance of our account will usually be paid to us when we terminate employment, for whatever reason.

Conversely, a defined benefit pension plan tends to favor older employees; employees in higher pay brackets; employees who have long years of service with the employer; and employees who quit their jobs after long years of service. These individual characteristics are so because a pension plan promises a definite benefit of retirement income with the level of contribution to be determined. Substantial benefits normally take years to accumulate.

Vesting

The *Employee Retirement Income Security Act of 1974* (ERISA), commonly referred to as the bible for employee benefit programs, features a requirement that a qualified retirement plan provide for **vesting** according to one of several schedules defined by law. **Vesting** means how much of the contributions or benefits accumulated on our behalf we will be allowed to keep, regardless of whether or not we stay with our current employer. If we leave the employ of our employer today, how much of the accumulated benefits or contributions will we own? Effective for qualified plan years beginning after December 31, 1988, the 1986 *Tax Reform Act* provides two alternative vesting schedules:

1. Five-year Cliff vesting, under which we would be 100 percent vested in employer-provided benefits or contributions after five years of service. If we terminate employment for reasons other than death or disability before we have accrued five years of service, we would not be eligible to receive benefits from the plan.
2. Three-year to seven-year vesting under which we would become vested in employer-provided benefits or contributions (see Table 3.1).

Table 3.1 Vesting Schedule

Years of Service	Percent Vesting
1	0%
2	0%
3	20%
4	40%
5	60%
6	80%
7 or more	100%

If our employer elects to follow a vesting schedule that would be of greater value to us, the IRS would approve. The two vesting schedules portray the strictest vesting schedules our employer may impose on us.

Concerning vesting rules and our plan, there are other general items of which we need to be aware. This is not an all-inclusive list, but simply some of the key rules. Keep in mind that this book is not intended to overwhelm you with details, but to simply raise your awareness. You can research any topic in this book by simply dropping by your local library. As to vesting rules, your plan must provide, among other things, that:

1. For profit-sharing and money purchase plans (defined contribution plans), separate accounting of your accrued benefit must be maintained. Further, separate accounting also needs to be maintained for permitted voluntary contributions.
2. No separate accounting is required for defined benefit plans except for our accrued benefit, which would result from permitted voluntary contributions.
3. Defined benefit and defined contribution plans must provide that all accrued benefits and contributions be fully vested upon termination of our plan by our employer.
4. Accrued benefits resulting from our own contributions can **never** be taken from us. These benefits are always 100% vested.
5. Any amendment changing the vesting schedule must give any plan participant who has three years or more of service, as of December 31, 1988, the right to have their vesting percentage computed without regard to the amendments.
6. If there is a merger or consolidation of a plan after the merger, we must be entitled to receive a benefit that is at least equal to the value of the benefit due us prior to the merger.
7. Benefit payments to a retiree or an employee who has separated from the employer cannot be decreased by increases in Social Security payments.

If we terminate our employ with our current employer and have vested interest in a plan or plans, a question is: "Should we take our vested interest, or leave it with our employer and file a claim for payment at some future date?" As a rule, it is generally wise to take what is due and payable to you, when it is due and payable. We can usually avoid current taxes if we complete a rollover to an Individual Retirement Account before 60 days lapses from the date we receive a distribution. This approach keeps our retirement assets under our control, not the control of our ex-employer.

Defined benefit plans tend to be employer pay all (noncontributory). With the rapid growth of salary reduction plans under section 401(k) of the IRC, there has been a significant growth in contributory plans—employees and employers both contribute. Employees commonly direct their investments within a framework provided by an investment committee appointed by the corporate board of directors. The 401(k) plan has become very popular with both employees and employers. Administration is simple and the plan has high visibility, since employees are participating and typically receive a monthly or quarterly statement as to the value of their account. There will continue to be significant growth in 401(k) plans and fewer defined benefit plans will be implemented in the future.

In comparing the defined benefit retirement plan with a defined contribution plan, we cannot ignore the cost/benefit differences. Under a defined benefit plan, the benefit is clearly defined up front, but the total cost is unknown. Cost can only be finalized under a defined benefit plan when the last participant covered under the plan dies. The employer retains this risk.

Under a defined contribution plan, the cost is clearly defined up front, but the benefit that we will be able to purchase at retirement is unknown. The participant in the defined contribution plan retains the risk.

Figure 3.1 depicts the flow of dollars and how it all works. Remember, each plan and trust, like the corporate entity, is a separate and unique legal entity standing alone. The vertical double lines represent that corporate contributions, when made, never return to the corporate entity.

In summary, the defined benefit income replacement approach is reasonably straightforward. This is because most defined benefit plans calculate the income replacement benefit on the basis of years of service and some average of our working years' salary. To determine the amount of income replacement under a defined contribution plan, determination or actual income is more difficult because there is no formula available to calculate the monthly benefit. It should be obvious then, that if we were to make an income replacement or a numerical comparison between defined benefit and defined contribution plans, we must rely heavily on assumptions in anticipating our future income.

These assumptions to calculate future income from a defined contribution plan would include (1) our starting salary, (2) the amount of yearly employer contribution, or combination of employer/employee contributions, (3) yearly increases, (4) years to retirement, and (5) earnings. Put another way; how much time do we have to invest? How much money do we have to invest? How much money can we earn from our investments? This is also called "time value of money." Risk for these assumptions are assumed by the individual participant. In determining

Figure 3.1

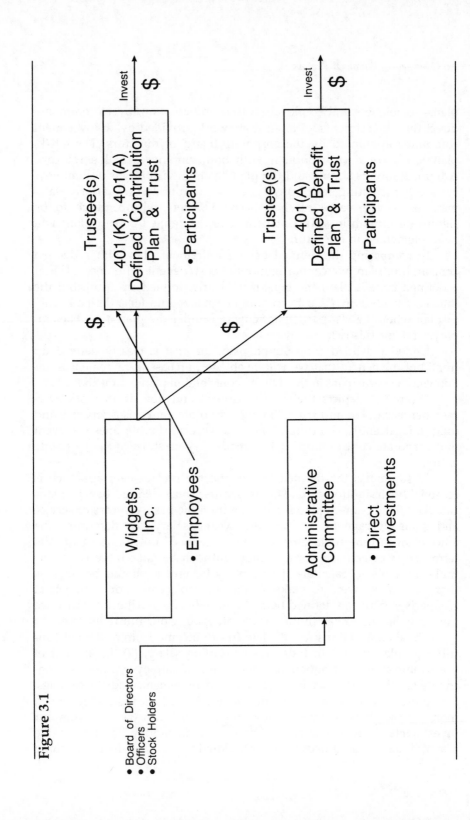

income replacement under a defined benefit method, similar assumptions are made by an actuary. In addition, the actuary includes labor force turnover, rates for disability, and life expectancy. Risk for defined benefit assumptions are assumed by the corporation. If the assumptions are wrong and adversely impact on the defined income replacement plan, then the corporation must contribute more money. If the results of these assumptions are positive, then the cost in providing income replacement is reduced to the corporation, resulting in a surplus. There can be no surplus in a defined contribution plan because any positive results are used to increase the individual participant's account. See Table 3.2, a comparison of defined benefit versus defined contribution income replacement plans.

Table 3.2 Comparison—Defined Benefit versus Defined Contribution

Income Replacement Plans

Provision	*Defined Benefit*	*Defined Contribution*
1. Eligibility	Age 21/1 year of service	Age 21/1 year of service
2. Normal Benefit	Years of service and salary	Uncertain—depends on years of participation, amount of money contributed, and earnings
3. Coverage	All employees	All employees
4. Risk Assumption	Employer	Individual plan participant
5. Early Benefit	Age (reduced benefit)	What you see is what you get—value of individual account
6. Inflation-index	Ad hoc	None
7. Funding	Accrued liability (advance funding)	Can be infrequent (not required) or flat percentage of pay
8. Accounting	Expenses accrued liability	Cash basis

(table continues)

Table 3.2 Comparison— Defined Benefit versus Defined Contribution (continued)

Provision	Defined Benefit	Defined Contribution
9. Vesting	Usually 5 year Cliff	Usually more rapid not uncommon to be 100% immediate
10. Individual accounts	Not maintained (money pooled)	Maintained by plan administrator
11. Actuarial calculations required	Yes	No
12. Pension Benefit Guaranty Corporation (PBGC) coverage (federal government)	Yes—on each active, retired, and terminated vested participant. Employer pays premium	No
13. Social Security integration	Common	Not common
14. Who pays	Generally the employer only (non-contributory)	Employer, employee (contributory) is common with the growth of 401(k) plans

Chapter 4

Health Care: Delivery Systems and You

You in the Health Care Arena

The five most common health care delivery vehicles in the United States today are:

1. "Doctor None, Coverage None"
2. Medicaid
3. Medicare
4. Managed Care Systems (HMOs, PPOs, EPOs, POSs)
5. Traditional Fee-For-Service Insurance

Each of these comes with a different price tag; will make different services available; and, will have different disadvantages and limitations.

Doctor None, Coverage None

This is the category in which you will be placed if you walk into the emergency room with some real medical problem but declare that you have no insurance and no regular physician. Unless you have cash available or it is clear that you may be retroactively approved for Medicaid, your fate will be determined by local custom, pertaining state law, and the charitable posture of the institution and physician. In other words, your care will be determined by luck. When I first started practice, in another town, a young female child was refused medical treatment and evaluation at two large hospitals after an alleged sexual assault. The need to transfer the child to a "charity" hospital delayed her care by some hours. In my present practice location, both major hospitals try to provide medical care to the indigent on the basis of need rather than on the ability to pay. So, *where* you get sick is important. In addition to the availability of care, "who" treats you (your doctor team) will be affected by your "Doctor None, Coverage None" status. In many locales, those people without insurance or with Medicaid will find themselves managed by medical students and residents under the guidance of fully trained staff physicians, whereas patients with insurance or greater means have a higher probability of being treated directly by the staff physician.

Who pays the cost of care given to "Doctor None, Coverage None" patients? We do. Governmental supported charity hospitals are supported directly by our taxes. Private institutions providing such care transfer the cost to us indirectly by charging patients with insurance more than the cost of their care to cover the cost of those who cannot pay. Twenty percent of hospitals in the United States are anticipated to go bankrupt by 1994—many of these because they will not be able to collect the cost of charity care that they provide.

Medicaid

Medicaid is a combined state and governmental assistance program created under Title XIX of the Social Security Trust Act. Its purpose is to provide health care for the poor and needy people of the United States. As a combined program, each state determines your income before Medicaid will help pay your medical and hospital bills. Eligibility standards and services provided are different in each Medicaid participating state.

Minimum Services Covered (Federal Guidelines)

1. Skilled nursing facility services for participants 21 or older; family planning services and supplies.
2. Physicians' services in their offices, your home, a hospital, clinic, care facility, or nursing home.
3. Home health services as an incentive to keep you in your home and out of institutions.
4. Inpatient hospital services. Excluded are psychiatric hospitals and institutions for the treatment of tuberculosis.
5. Outpatient hospital services as long as a physician supervises your case.
6. Laboratory and x-ray services.

The inclusion of any other medical services is up to each state.

As a Minimum—Who Is Eligible (Federal Guidelines)

The following categories of needy must be able to get Medicaid protection from their state:

1. All people who are not receiving SSI (Supplemental Security Income) or AFDC (Aid to Families with Dependent Children).
2. All families receiving AFDC.
3. All people receiving welfare payments under an SSI type of program.

The entire mandatory coverage requirement is tied to SSI and AFDC.

If you qualify for Medicare but cannot afford all the deductibles, premiums, and copayments that Medicare doesn't pay, you can apply for assistance from Medicaid. Remember, you do not have to be covered by Social Security to be eligible for Medicaid.

Who pays for Medicaid? We do through federal, state, and local tax dollars.

How to Apply for Medicaid

Go to either your Social Security office or your local office of the State Social Services Department, Department of Public Assistance, or Welfare Department.

Medicare

Medicare is a federal system to compensate hospitals (Part A) and physicians (Part B) for health care to certain segments of the population, the elderly, and the disabled. The system is divided into:

Part A: Hospital coverage—financed on a pay-as-you-go basis from Social Security Taxes

Part B: Physician and outpatient coverage—25 percent of funds come from premiums of eligible patients and 75 percent of funds come from general revenue.

The cost of Medicare is borne by us through our Social Security Taxes with a portion of "Part B" being supported by general revenue from our Federal Income Tax. At present, 2.9 percent of our income up to a salary of $125,000 per year (as taxable by Social Security) goes to the Medicare fund. Obviously, the amount of money contributed to the Medicare fund will depend upon the amount of taxes paid. The amount of taxes paid, in turn, depends upon the strength of the economy—how many of us are employed or unemployed and how much money we make. The money is collected and dispensed on a pay-as-you-go basis. That is, people who pay into the system are paying for eligible Americans who are sick now. They do not "bank" any money for their own possible illness in future years. This could lead to difficult problems in a population that is aging because we have more older Americans entitled to receive benefits but fewer younger Americans to contribute for their care. The board of trustees of the Federal Hospital Insurance Fund has predicted in their annual report that Medicare will be broke before 1995 even in a strong economy. Expect some changes in Medicare funding or in the provision for services offered.

Hospital reimbursement is presently based on the **DRG System** (Diagnostic Related Groups). When a patient enters a hospital, he or she is assigned a diagnostic category that determines how much the hospital will be reimbursed. The payment is unrelated to the actual cost of care. There is an appeals system for very unusual patients called "outliers."

Physician reimbursement is generally on a fee-for-service basis, but Medicare pays less for services than the physician would usually receive in the free marketplace.

Managed Care Systems (HMOs, etc.)

Managed care systems were established in the United States with the goal of providing an efficient means of health care delivery at reduced cost. The founders of managed care systems realized that traditionally the more health care a vendor sold, the richer he became because he sent you a bill and you paid it. The incentive was to be generous in dispensing care. Managed care advocates believed that in a prepaid environment that the incentive would be reversed. The less health care given, the more subscriber dollars kept as profit. The more health care administered, the poorer the vendor becomes. This system breeds efficiency, fewer hospital days per population segment; and the avoidance, as much as possible, of expensive highly specialized care and referral.

Enter the HMO

The essence of the HMO system is that subscriber health care dollars are paid to salaried (or capitated) physicians with the agreement that these physicians will provide health care as it is needed to the subscribers. The prototype HMO is the large Kaiser Permanente Group based in California. They have earned the reputation for delivering solid "no frills" care to their participants. Now, there are many plans throughout the United States.

As good as the concept might seem, there are some disadvantages to the system:

1. It limits your choice of physicians to plan participants.
2. The HMO prospers and its physicians are rewarded as less health care is dispensed. This is the inverse of the traditional value of rewarding greater productivity.
3. Getting sick away from home can be a problem.
4. Obtaining referral for a specialist may not be as easy as in conventional plans.
5. If you contract a very unusual disease, you are more likely to be treated locally than to be referred to a world expert who practices some distance away from you.

Taking these factors into consideration, the best time to belong to an HMO is when you are young and healthy and have young healthy children.

Many HMOs have programs of preventive care that teach good health habits if you *participate* in them. Access to family practitioners and pediatricians is relatively inexpensive. When families are young, they are less likely to need expensive, complex treatments.

Traditional Fee-For-Service Insurance

You pay your health insurance company and they invest the money. When you get sick and require physician or hospital services, the insurance company picks up the tab for all covered items. (It is important to read your contract before signing so you know you have good coverage.) This is the simplest, the oldest, and many feel the best (and perhaps a soon to be extinct) form of **fee-for-service** health insurance.

The fees you pay will be determined by the "pool at risk" (i.e., the number, age, condition of health, and health care utilization rate of those in the group insured). Many feel it is the best because there is no disincentive to refer. If you need a specialist to evaluate you or need a complex operation, your physician refers you and your insurance pays. You have access to the "best" when you need it. Many feel it will soon be extinct. As managed and alternative health care plans take young healthy folks from the risk pool, the cost of caring for those left will drive the premiums out of sight.

There is another less obvious factor driving up the cost of traditional insurance. As "Doctor None, Coverage None" patients receive care, this is paid for by charging private patients more to cover their cost. As the government reimburses hospitals for Medicare patients less than the cost of their care, a loss is incurred. This loss can be recovered in one of two ways. First, we can withhold care from the elderly who are very sick. Or second, we can "shift" those losses to private payers. As hospitals "cost shift" to traditional fee-for-service payers, fee-for-service policies become so expensive that for all practical purposes they cease to exist.

The major drawback of traditional plans is that you will be sold too much health care. Unlike managed care, vendors prosper with utilization. Therefore, the buyers must beware. In the age of tight health care dollars, there is tremendous pressure from insurance carriers, hospital utilization review committees, and third party case managers to keep dispensed health care down. So, even with the best insurance, the weight of concern is that Americans will receive less health care than they need due to the cost burden.

Retiree Health Care: The Financial Accounting Standards Board Challenges the Tradition of Public-Private Sector Cooperation— Statement 106

As a rule, corporate boards of directors are keenly aware and sensitive to the security needs of employees. This is particularly true for income replacement and health care needs during retirement. For the past several decades, it has been common policy, especially for larger companies, to provide health care coverage to those employees who have retired and are eligible for Medicare. This coverage is commonly referred to as **Medi-Gap** or "retiree health care benefits," depending on the "richness" of the program being offered by the corporation. This means that the corporation will pay for their retiree's health care needs not provided under Medicare.

Over the years, this practice has been viewed by top corporate management as being responsible to the individual and a good citizen of the community. Such generosity in this manner is okay if justified. It's good for the corporate image, good for the retiree, good for the employee looking forward to retirement, and good for local community and governing agencies.

Recently, the *Financial Accounting Standards Board* (FASB) issued *Statement 106*, which will change the way employees and corporations must account for Post-Retirement Benefits Other Than Pensions. Number 106 requires companies to recognize benefit costs and liabilities as they are incurred. It requires companies to record unfunded retiree health benefit liabilities on their financial statements (balance sheet). The new accounting rules take effect beginning with fiscal years after December 15, 1991.

What is the estimated incurred liabilities? No one knows. If we knew the cost, we'd step right up. Who can predict the future? The government itself is a major determinant in providing health care for the retiree. Government policy can and does change overnight, depending on current events as viewed by the political mind. Estimations of incurred cost have been from 250 billion to one trillion dollars. Take a number. What will health care cost be in the future? Take a number.

What is important for all of us to keep in mind about *Statement 106* is that it relates to all post-retirement benefits except pensions and that it applies to current and future retirees, their beneficiaries, and qualified dependents.

A little background about retiree health benefits is necessary. This benefit was originally offered in the 1940s and 1950s when business was booming as a result of economic expansion. The United States was the only major industrialized nation not devastated by World War II. There were very few retirees in relation to the number of active workers. Today, all that has changed. We have increasing life spans, changing demographics of the work force, and rising health care cost. The retiree-to-active worker ratio and the retiree health care liabilities have increased enormously.

What can we expect the future to hold for retiree health care plans and plan design? There are several possibilities and the most obvious ones are:

1. Corporations will drop retiree health care coverage for all future retirees.
2. There will be no changes in retiree health care coverage. Corporations now offering retiree health coverage to their employees will simply absorb the cost (pass on to the consumer), comply with *Statement 106* and classify it as the cost of "doing business" in this current massive legislative environment.
3. Corporations will place a CAP on post-retirement medical promises.
4. Corporations will tie promise for post-retirement health care coverage to length of employment.
5. Corporations will establish an advance funding program and require the employee to contribute starting with the date of their hire.
6. Corporations will establish some combination of the possibilities.

If we expect to live beyond a subsistence level, we will need more money during our retirement years than any previous generation in our history. Because of our burgeoning national debt and aging population, we will be forced to face continual inflation, increased taxes, rising health care costs, and means testing for social security and government health care benefit programs. When should we start planning for the "golden years"? It's never too soon. For all of us the answer is yesterday. Future generations must pay for political decisions of the past.

Part III

Chapter 5

Retirement Systems in the United States: Securing the Future— Income Replacement Programs

Qualified Pension Plans

To be a **Qualified Pension Plan,** our employer must adhere to certain requirements legislated by Congress and administered by three agencies—the U.S. Department of Labor (DOL), the Internal Revenue Service (IRS), and the Pension Benefit Guaranty Corporation (PBGC). Why all of these legislation and government agencies? Simply put, it's because of the many past instances of workers losing their retirement benefits as a result of the actions of senior corporate management. The most notable of such actions took place in 1963 when 4,000 Studebaker auto workers lost some or all of their promised benefits. Congress, in 1974, took measures to prevent such tragedies by enacting the *Employee Retirement Income Securities Act* (ERISA). What does ERISA do? Among other things, ERISA:

1. Sets standards of conduct for those who manage plan assets.
2. Requires that funds be regularly contributed to provide for promised pension benefits (advance funding).
3. Ensures that we are entitled to receive our pension benefits after we have satisfied minimum requirements.
4. Makes certain that we and our beneficiaries are provided with adequate and comprehensible information about our pension plan.
5. Provides a pension insurance program administered by PBGC that guarantees that we will receive certain basic benefits even if our defined benefit plan is terminated with insufficient assets to pay our promised benefits.
6. Mandates the way pension plans must operate to be "tax-qualified."

Along these same lines, ERISA states that a pension plan must be operated solely in the interest of participants and beneficiaries. Pension funds must be held in a trust fund or insurance policies. These must be used exclusively to provide benefits for plan participants. With few exceptions, these funds may not be returned to the employer while the plan is in operation.

It is important that we make a distinction between a trust and the plan. We hear income replacement programs referred to as:

- Retirement trust
- Retirement plans
- Pension trust
- Retirement plan and trust, and
- Pension plan and trust

Often those who use such terms do so with little understanding of their precise meanining. A **trust** holds the money. The trust receives, accounts for, and disburses the assets of the trust. A **trustee** is that person or organization who has been hired or appointed by the corporate board of directors to receive, to account for, and to disburse funds. The trust document, usually written by an attorney, states the trustee's authority.

On the other hand, a **plan** specifies all of the necessary administrative procedures and requirements. The plan covers such things as who is eligible to participate in the plan and trust, the vesting schedule, the benefit or contribution formula, the survivor benefits, the disability procedures, and so forth. The board of directors appoints a plan administrator who is responsible for the plan conforming with the Internal Revenue Code (IRC) regulating the plan.

So, we can simply state that a trust holds the money, and a plan deals with the daily operational administrative requirements. Furthermore, the trustee is responsible for the money, and the plan administrator is responsible for administration and conformity with ERISA.

Once a plan is determined to be "qualified," income replacement benefits for plan participants are not taxable until they are distributed from the trust. Employer contributions to fund these benefits are a deductible expense, within limits, as soon as contributed to the trust. (Remember, the trust is where the money is deposited, accounted for, and dispersed.) Assets in the trust earn investment income on a tax-deferred basis.

In order for the corporation to retain this favorable tax policy, it cannot provide excessive benefits to highly paid employees and minimal benefits to low- and middle-income employees. Therefore, the plan must maintain certain levels of coverage and cannot discriminate by paying higher benefits to highly paid employees or owners of the company. For purposes of comparing benefits, the employer may take into account the Social Security contributions and/or benefits that he or she provides through FICA taxes, to the extent permitted under the Internal Revenue Code. Plans that take benefits provided by the employer through the Social Security system are known as **integrated plans**. We've all heard and read stories about the chairman of the board of corporation X who retires with an annual retirement income in excess of one million dollars. This level of benefit is not coming from a qualified income replacement plan and trust. This level of income replacement is coming from a "nonqualified deferred compensation" arrangement that obligates future corporate earnings to this "super-human" who has arguably done so much for the corporation during his or her tenure. In many cases it is not the chairman of the board, but some senior executive officer who receives such a sweetheart deal. Most of us don't have to worry about dealing with such generosity.

A reasonable question is "can the employer end (terminate) a pension plan and trust"? The answer to that is "yes," but in the case of a defined benefit plan and trust, only if they meet safeguards designed to protect the plan participants. This can be accomplished either through a standard termination or a distress termination.

Standard Termination

A **standard termination** can occur only if the plan has enough assets to pay all benefit liabilities. Termination may not proceed until the plan administrator delivers a written "Notice of Intent to Terminate" the plan to each participant, beneficiary, and the employees' union. This must be done at least 60 days before the proposed termination date. In addition, the plan administrator must issue a second notice, the "Notice of Plan Benefits," to each plan participant or beneficiary of a deceased participant. This notice, written in plain language, must provide the benefit amount and the essential information used to determine each person's benefit entitlement, such as date of birth, salary history, and years of service.

The plan administrator must also file a separate notice with PBGC, as soon as possible after the 60-day notice to the participants. This notice includes basic data about the plan, an enrolled actuary's certification that the plan has sufficient assets to pay all benefit liabilities, and the plan administrator's certification of the accuracy of the information used in terminating the plan.

After receiving the notice of standard termination, PBGC has 60 days to review the termination to make certain that it complies with all legal requirements. If the termination does not comply, PBGC will issue a "Notice of Non-Compliance." Otherwise, as soon as practicable after PBGC's 60-day review period expires, the plan administrator must pay the benefit liabilities in full by purchasing annuities from an insurance company or in some cases lump-sum payments may be made as an alternative form of distribution. Within 30 days after the assets are distributed, the plan administrator must send PBGC a notice certifying that the assets have been distributed as required.

Distress Termination

In **distress termination**, if a plan lacks sufficient funds to pay all of its benefit liabilities, it may not be terminated until and unless PBGC determines that the plan's sponsor can meet at least one of the four distress tests:

1. Chapter 7 bankruptcy liquidation, or a similar state insolvency proceeding.
2. Chapter 11 bankruptcy reorganization, or a similar state proceeding, provided that the bankruptcy court or other appropriate court determines that the employer will be unable to pay all of its debts pursuant to a plan of reorganization and will be unable to continue in business outside the reorganization process unless the pension plan is terminated.
3. PBGC determines that, unless a distress termination occurs, the employer will be unable to pay its debts when due and continue in business.
4. PBGC determines that the costs of providing pension coverage have become unreasonably burdensome solely as a result of a decline in the work force covered as participants in all single-employer plans of the employer.

In a distress termination, the plan administrator must issue a written "Notice of Intent to Terminate" to PBGC, participants, beneficiaries, and other affected parties at least 60 days in advance of the proposed termination date of the plan.

If a plan qualifies for distress termination and can pay all of its benefit liabilities, PBGC will authorize the plan administrator to distribute the assets and complete the termination as in a standard termination. If the plan cannot pay all of its benefit liabilities, the plan administrator may be authorized to distribute the assets or PBGC may assign trustees to the trust. These trustees include one to handle all incoming funds, and the second trustee to handle all out-going funds. PBGC will use its insurance funds to the extent necessary to pay the plan participants their guaranteed benefits. The employer then becomes liable to PBGC for unpaid contributions and for unfunded benefit liability. The PBGC will then receive whatever they can get from the remaining assets of the corporation.

Under a qualified income replacement plan, is our money protected from financial losses caused by mismanagement and misuse of assets through its fiduciary provisions? This leads us to confront fiduciary responsibility.

What is a fiduciary? According to the dictionary, a **fiduciary** is a person who occupies a position of trust, one who holds or controls property for the benefit of another person. Taken further, ERISA defines a fiduciary as anyone who exercises discretionary control or authority over plan management or assets, anyone with discretionary authority or responsibility in the administration of a plan, or anyone who provides investment advice to a plan for compensation or has any authority or responsibility to do so. Included in the definition then, would be plan trustees, plan administrators, members of a plan's investment committee, and generally, persons who select these individuals (board of directors). What kind of protection does the fiduciary requirement provide? The fiduciary provisions:

1. Outline the duties of fiduciaries.
2. Prohibit certain transactions.
3. Require that our benefit plans be established and maintained under a written instrument and that provision be made for one or more named fiduciaries with authority to control and manage the operation and administration of the plan.
4. Require that the assets of our benefit plans, with some exception, be held in trust unless the assets consist of insurance or annuity contracts.
5. Require bonding of all persons who handle funds or property of a plan to provide protection against plan losses through fraud or dishonesty.
6. Prohibit persons convicted of certain crimes from serving in specified positions with respect to our benefit plans for a stipulated period of time.

There are four general fiduciary duties. A fiduciary must:

1. Discharge his or her duties solely in the interest of plan participants and beneficiaries and for the exclusive purpose of providing plan benefits to them and defraying the reasonable expenses of administering the plan.
2. Act with care, skill, prudence, and diligence under the circumstances then prevailing that a "prudent person" acting in like capacity and familiar with such matters would use in the conduct of an enterprise of a like character and with like aims (income replacement).

3. Diversify plan investments in order to minimize the risk of large losses unless it is clearly prudent not to do so.
4. Operate in accordance with plan documents and instruments.

In order to prevent conflicts of interest and self-dealing, fiduciaries are barred from a number of prohibited transactions and activities. A fiduciary may not:

1. Be paid for his or her services if he or she is already receiving full-time pay from an employer or union whose employees or members are participants.
2. Act in any capacity involving the plan on behalf of a party whose interests are adverse to the interests of the plan, its participants, or its beneficiaries.
3. Receive any consideration for his or her personal account from any party dealing with the plan in connection with a transaction involving plan assets.
4. Permit the investment to exceed 10 percent of plan assets in certain securities of the employer or of a substantial affiliation of the employer or certain real property leased to the employer (except in the case of profit sharing plans, stock bonus, thrift or savings, employee stock ownership plans, and certain money purchase plans).
5. Cause a plan to engage in a transaction with a "party in interest" if the transaction involves, directly or indirectly, sale, exchange, or lease of property; lending money or extending credit; furnishing goods, services or facilities; or transfer of assets to or use of assets by or for the benefit of a party in interest.

A fiduciary who breaches any responsibility or duty under ERISA may be personally liable to make good any losses to the plan resulting from such a breach and to restore to the plan any profits made through improper use of plan assets. A fiduciary is also subject to such other equitable or remedial relief as a court may deem appropriate, including removal.

You may be wondering who is a party of interest. **Parties in interest** (called "disqualified persons" in the Internal Revenue Code) include:

- Any administrator, officer, trustee, custodian, counsel, or employee of a plan

- A fiduciary
- Any person providing services to a plan
- The employer of covered employees
- An employee organization whose members are covered
- An owner, direct or indirect, of 50 percent or more of the company
- Certain relatives of parties of interest
- Certain other affiliated corporations, employees, officers, directors, partners, and joint-ventures

ERISA provides some exemptions to the prohibited transactions provisions. For example, loans by the plan to parties in interest who are participants or beneficiaries are generally permitted if they are available on a nondiscriminatory basis, bear a reasonable rate of interest, are adequately secured, and are made in accordance with the plan rules. Likewise, under certain conditions, arrangements with a party in interest for office space or legal, accounting, or other necessary services for the plan are permitted if no more than a reasonable compensation is paid.

When did all of this become effective? The year was 1975, one year after the implementation of ERISA—1974. Has Congress overreacted to the "Studebaker problem"? The answer to that question is "yes." Employers are overwhelmed with annual legislation that all too frequently requires that trust and plan documents be amended (many refer to these legislative changes as the "annual attorney's relief act"). Penalties for noncompliance can be substantial. Congress has created a gigantic administrative nightmare since ERISA was legislated in 1974. There is no relief for the immediate future. There is some talk in the halls of Congress concerning pension and welfare plans simplification. Experience indicates that simplification normally translates to mean revenue enhancement to the federal government. We'll wait and see if future simplification legislation is a reality or a figment of someone's imagination. One approach toward simplification is to change the option, without penalty, to withdraw income replacement funds from age 59 1/2 to age 59, and mandatory withdrawal starting at age 70 1/2 to age 70.

These changes will excite no one except members of Congress. Furthermore, the discussion revolves around removal of ten- and five-year income averaging for lump sum distributions. In other words, no matter how we receive our funds from a retirement plan, it will be taxed as ordinary income. The result of such legislation will be to enhance the flow of money to Congress while removing more retirement funds from our pockets. This is all done under the title of "plan simplification." We never want to forget the *Tax Reform Act of 1986*. Congress clearly "marketed" and communicated to us that this legislation was a tax reduction and tax simplification. Today, who among us believes such nonsense?

Defined Benefit Plans

A **defined benefit plan** provides a definitely determinable annual benefit. The level of benefit received at retirement is clearly stated, with contributions to be determined. An actuary determines the required employer contribution each year, taking into account the level of benefit formula and certain economic and noneconomic factors. Among the most common of these factors are investment return, salary increases, Social Security wage base, cost of living increases, and administrative expenses. Other factors include rates of death, turnover, and disability.

The most common types of defined benefit plans are: fixed benefit plans, flat benefit plans, and unit benefit plans.

Fixed Benefit Plans

We, as participants in the **fixed benefit plan**, would receive a level monthly payment regardless of differences in compensation or years of service with our employer. We would be entitled to a monthly pension, starting at normal retirement date, and payable for life, for example, of $300 each and every month. Such a payment would be an example of a typical formula used in a fixed benefit plan. For obvious reasons the fixed benefit plan formula is seldom used.

Flat Benefit Plans

The benefit payable to us in a **flat benefit plan** depends entirely upon our level of compensation. A typical formula used in a flat benefit plan might be: each participant shall be entitled to a monthly pension, commencing at normal retirement date, payable for life, of an amount equal to 40 percent of our monthly compensation. Under this benefit method, if our monthly income is $1,000, we would receive a monthly pension of $400; if our monthly compensation is $2,000, we would receive a monthly pension of twice as much, or $800.

Unit Benefit Plans

The **unit benefit plan** type of plan acknowledges service with a company by providing greater benefits for a long service employee than for a short-term employee with the same average salary. A type of formula used under the unit benefit plan might be: each participant shall be entitled to a monthly pension, starting at normal retirement date, payable for life, of an amount equal to 1 percent of our monthly base pay multiplied by our years of service with the company. Under this formula, if our monthly pay was $2,000 and we have 30 years of employment at our retirement date, then we would receive $600 (1% x $2,000 = $20 x 30 years of service = $600); while an employee with the same monthly pay but only ten years of employment, will receive $200 (1% x $2,000 = $20 x 10 years of service = $200).

The unit benefit plan is by far the most common benefit method used in the United States when a defined benefit plan has been adopted by a company. Each of these examples reflects a formula that is not integrated with Social Security. Once Social Security integration is considered, the differences become more important.

Profit-Sharing Plans

In a **profit-sharing plan**, contributions are based on the profits or the earnings of our company. The level of contribution is normally determined each year depending on the plan formula. A question that may come to mind might be: "Need my employer have profits in order to make a qualified contribution to a profit-sharing plan"? The answer is "no." However, it stands to reason that if we work for a private sector for-profit company, if there is no profit there is nothing from which to make contributions. A tax-exempt organization cannot establish and make contributions to a profit-sharing plan. Maximum annual contributions is the lesser of 15 percent of our annual salary, or $30,000 per individual participant account, subject to future cost of living adjustments.

Money Purchase Pension Plans

Money purchase pension plans are different from profit-sharing plans to the extent that contributions are usually made regardless of profits. The specific contribution formula is set forth in the plan document.

Maximum annual contribution is the lesser of 25 percent of our annual salary or $30,000 per individual account, subject to future cost of living adjustments.

If our company has a combination of profit-sharing and money purchase pension plans (which is common), the combined maximum annual contribution is the lesser of 25 percent of our annual salary, or $30,000 per individual participant account, subject to future cost of living increases.

Salary Reduction—401(k) IRC

If our employer offers us an opportunity to participate in a **Cash or Deferred Arrangement** (CODA), also known as **Salary Reduction Plan**, and probably more commonly known as a 401(k) plan, we should participate. We should save as much as we possibly can and still maintain our household. There are a few programs available to us that permit:

- Contributions to be tax deductible
- Earnings to accumulate on a tax-deferred basis
- Possibility of special income tax averaging when we withdraw our money at retirement

In addition, at retirement we can roll all or part of our accumulation into an IRA account and continue the tax-deferred build-up until age 70 1/2. Furthermore, a salary reduction plan is a sound disciplined savings program because our employer collects our contribution and makes all deposits for us. We are also the happy recipient of an immediate reduction in state and federal taxes paid, since our payroll department calculates our taxes after deductible contributions have been made. A 401(k) plan is a **defined contribution plan.**

What are the restrictions to our use of this money? The plan provides that contributions may not be distributed to us before the earliest of the following events:

- Death
- Disability
- Retirement
- Termination of employment
- Attaining age 59 1/2 or
- Hardship

Distribution for Hardship

Effective December 31, 1988, a **hardship distribution** is one which is necessary in light of immediate and heavy financial needs. Furthermore, these needs cannot be reasonably satisfied from other resources. The decision of financial need must be made in accordance with uniform and nondiscriminatory standards set forth in the plan. The hardship distribution cannot exceed the amount required to meet the immediate financial need. Our plan will be permitted to distribute only our elective contributions, but no earnings on those contributions. Employer-matching contributions and non-elective contributions may not be distributed on account of hardship. If we are younger than 59 1/2, the 10% will apply to the amount distributed, plus we will be required to include the distribution as ordinary income in the taxable year that we received the funds.

The maximum elective contribution we may make to a 401(k) plan is approximately $8,728 per year. This current cap will be increased based on future cost of living adjustments.

A 401(k) plan is a solid employee benefit program. To reap its full benefit, we must apply ourselves to understanding how it works and what it can do for us. Get involved and stay involved. New legislation is published frequently. Your local library has the latest changes, as well as your company benefits specialist.

Cash Balance Pension Plans

The **cash balance pension plan** is an innovative approach in attempting to solve an old problem: how to effectively communicate a defined benefit plan, with all of its complicated formulas, to the plan participants. The purported answer is to have a defined benefit plan but operate and communicate the plan as if it were a defined contribution plan. In fact, some sponsors of cash balance plans think of it like a bank account with benefits expressed in dollars and cents.

The question we might ask is "How is this done?" It is done by offering the following easy to understand features:

1. A dollar amount based on years of service is credited each month to an account in our name.
2. Interest is credited to our account each quarter.

3. Quarterly statements show the growth of our account and provides high visibility—similar to a 401(k) defined contribution plan.
4. Rapid vesting of our employer's contributions.
5. Our benefit is portable; that is, we take the vested portion of our account with us if we leave the company before retirement. Most defined benefit plans do not provide for portability unless the present value at the time of termination is less than $3,500.
6. At retirement, we can select between a single lump sum payment, or lifetime monthly payment. Most defined benefit plans provide only for lifetime monthly payments. Generally, if the participant is married at the time of retirement, a joint and survivor annuity must be taken unless the nonparticipant spouse signs a written, notarized consent to choose a lump-sum distribution or an annuity that does not provide continuing payments to our spouse following death.

Under a cash balance plan, the employer normally makes all contributions just like most defined benefit plans operating in the United States. Remember, a cash balance plan is a defined benefit plan disguised as a defined contribution plan. The participant does not bear the risk of investment loss—the employer does. In a defined contribution plan, the participant bears the risk of investment loss. Excess earnings usually reduce employer contributions.

In a cash balance pension plan, benefits must be available in annuity form, and consequently the plan must specify the actuarial factors used to convert the account balances to the various annuity options of benefit.

Cash balance pension plans are also known as:

- Account balance plan
- Guaranteed account balance plan
- Cash account pension plan and
- Pension equivalent reserve credit

Cash balance plans tend to be expensive to operate. The adopting company is required to comply with all defined benefit and defined contribution procedures, not just for one plan, but for two plans.

Chapter 6

Individual Income Replacement Programs

Individual Retirement Account (IRA)

IRA (**individual retirement account**)—these three letters stared out from bank and savings and loans display counters, mutual funds ads, newspaper ads, insurance company literature, and stockbroker standard sales material. The contributory IRA was a sound program that provided enough of a tax incentive to encourage a great number of Americans to invest in their future security. It appeared to be a "win-win" program; namely, a program that was good politically, economically, and socially for our society. Yet, Congress has reneged.

Today, the banners are down, the ads are seldom displayed, and few Americans qualify to continue with their contributions and tax deductions for this program. The *Tax Reform Act of 1986*, effective January 1, 1987, guaranteed the return of the contributory IRA to a low profile, with few Americans eligible to participate. Under the new rules, those tax payers who are eligible can seldom afford to contribute.

Who Is Eligible?

First, to have an IRA we must receive earned income. From our monetary arena discussion, we know that earned income is that income (such as wages, salaries, or professional fees) that flows into our household from business as a return for our labor or services. Alimony is considered to be earned income for IRA purposes.

If we are age 70 1/2, our IRA contribution days are over. No contributions can be made to a contributory IRA and no deduction is allowed for the taxable year in which we turn 70 1/2 and for each year after 70 1/2. If we are single and have an adjusted gross income (AGI) of $25,000 or less, we are eligible to contribute up to $2,000 into our individual retirement plan. If we are covered by a qualified retirement plan at our place of employment, we will lose $200 of deduction for every $1,000 our AGI exceeds $25,000. Put another way, for every $5 of earnings in excess of AGI $25,000, we lose $1 of IRA deductions. Our deduction becomes a wash at $35,000. If we are single and not covered by a qualified retirement plan at our place of employment, and AGI is $2,000 or more (meaning no cap on the level of income), we are eligible to contribute up to a maximum level of $2,000 as provided for under *Sections 408* and *415* of the Internal Revenue Code (IRC).

If we are married and file a joint income tax return and have a combined gross income of $40,000 or less, we are eligible to make a contribution of $2,000. If both we and our spouse have earned income, each with a minimum of $2,000, then each of us can contribute $2,000 to our respective individual retirement accounts. If we file a joint return and our combined adjusted gross income is $40,000 or less, we would be eligible to contribute to and deduct for a spousal individual retirement account. This tactic will increase our contribution level and deduction to $2,250. Remember, two accounts must be opened, each in the name of the respective spouse. No single account opened in this manner can receive a contribution for less than $250. Now, assume both work and have an adjusted gross income in excess of $40,000. For every $1,000 of earnings over $40,000, the couple will each lose $200 of contribution and deduction. Our deduction and contribution would be a wash at $50,000 of adjusted gross income. This is assuming that one or both spouses, it matters not which one, is a participant and covered by a qualified retirement plan through their employer. If both spouses work, and neither is a participant under a qualified retirement plan at their respective places of employment, then whatever the amount of their adjusted gross income, each would be eligible to contribute $2,000 to their respective individual retirement accounts.

Funds contributed to an IRA are not available until age 59 1/2 without paying a 10 percent penalty and including the amount distributed as ordinary income in the year distribution is made. This 10 percent penalty is classified as an "early withdrawal" from an IRA.

Generally, we can receive IRA distributions before age 59 1/2 without paying the 10 percent penalty tax on premature distributions when:

- Death occurs (this is the hard way).
- We become disabled.
- We receive our money in periodic payments for our life or the joint lives of ourselves and our beneficiary. Such claims cannot be paid less frequently than annually. Furthermore, this election could only be made after we separate from service with our employer.
- Divorce proceedings directed by the courts.
- Medical expenses, but then only to the exact amount of such expenses not covered by other health care plans in which we might participate, and must exceed 7 1/2 percent of our adjusted gross income (AGI). What does 7 1/2 percent really mean? It means that for every $10,000 of AGI, $750 is not deductible as a medical expense. This was passed by Congress under the *Tax Reform Act of 1986*.

Ordinary income will always be payable for the year in which distribution from our IRA is made, regardless of reason.

In summary, when setting up an IRA account be aware that:

1. Accounts must be held by a trust or in a custodial account. The holder or trustee must be a bank, savings and loan, insured credit union, or trust company. An individual cannot be trustee.
2. Accounts may not invest in collectibles, in life insurance or an endowment contract. After December 31, 1986, IRAs may acquire gold or silver coins issued by the United States.
3. If an IRA is used as security for a loan, it is not necessarily disqualified. The amount used as security is treated as distributed from the account, subject to taxes and penalties.

Nondeductible IRAs

There is no question that the *Tax Reform Act of 1986* has changed the availability of IRAs for most investors. The concept of deductibility of contributions from current income, and the deferral of taxes on earnings, is still very appealing. What has changed is that the act has made contributions to IRAs nondeductible from current income for a rather large percentage of taxpayers. The change will have significant impact on our planning strategy in providing for long-term security requirements. Many Americans who qualify to contribute to an IRA can't afford to do so.

If we are covered by our employer's pension plan, the deduction of IRA contributions is a function of our adjusted gross income. The *Tax Reform Act of 1986* eliminated deductions for IRA contributions if our AGI (before IRA contributions) exceeds $50,000 if we're married and filing a joint return, and $35,000 if we're single. The entire $2,000 deduction from current income is available to us if our AGI is less than $40,000 for married couples filing a joint return, and $25,000 if we're single. Put another way, our deduction is reduced by $1 for every $5 of income that falls in the "in between" zone.

So we don't qualify to make a deductible contribution. What now? We could still make a $2,000 nondeductible contribution to our IRA. This strategy would allow us to defer taxes on interest earnings. Upon withdrawal, taxes would apply only to that portion representing earnings. The penalty for early withdrawal (prior to 59 1/2) remains, but applies only to the portion that represents earnings. If we took a partial withdrawal prior to age 59 1/2, the amount subject to penalty and tax is the prorated earnings based on the percentage of the total represented by earnings.

As a rule, the benefits of a nondeductible IRA are greater for longer holding periods, higher annual rates of interest, and higher personal tax rates.

The adverse impact of the withdrawal penalty makes the nondeductible IRA unattractive for taxpayers needing the money before age 59 1/2. The risk is that the money will be unexpectedly needed and withdrawn before age 59 1/2. Such an event could prove to be very costly to us. We could suffer through three penalties: (1) the financial institution where our money is invested may very well impose a penalty—it's their "policy" to do so; (2) 10 percent penalty for withdrawal prior to age 59 1/2; (3) inclusion of a portion of the amount withdrawn as ordinary income for the taxable year we elected the early withdrawal option.

Now, consider the record keeping requirements for us, the taxpayer. The original contribution that we make to a nondeductible IRA is not taxed upon withdrawal, while it is for a deductible IRA. If we have both a deductible IRA and nondeductible IRA, any withdrawals are considered to have come from both in the same proportion that each represents of the total. If our records are unclear or incomplete as to how much of the total the nondeductible IRA represents, the IRS will certainly treat the entire amount as having come from the deductible IRA. In other words, we will be taxed on the entire amount as we withdraw and use the funds. Our record keeping must be exact.

For the Self-Employed Person—Keogh (HR-10) Plan

If we are the sole proprietor of an unincorporated business, or partner who owns more than 10 percent of either the capital interest or the profit interest in the partnership, then we are a self-employed owner employee.

One of the retirement delivery systems available to us, as a sole proprietor, is commonly referred to as a **Keogh plan** or an HR-10 plan. The plan was named after Congressman Keogh, a congressional representative from the New England area, who introduced retirement legislation for the self-employed in the early 1960s. This legislation became House of Representatives Bill 10, hence the HR-10 tag.

The basic tax advantages for adopting an HR-10 plan are that our contributions to this qualified retirement plan are tax-deductible and the earnings are allowed to accumulate on a tax-deferred basis. Furthermore, special 10-year/5-year forward income averaging may be available at retirement if we elect to take a lump-sum distribution. 10-year/5-year forward income averaging is not available for IRAs.

Currently, Congress is proposing to eliminate special taxes for lump-sum distributions received from corporate 401(a) plans, 401(k) plans, and Keogh plans. Under the umbrella of tax simplification, Congress wants to tax all income distributions as ordinary income. Congress takes more, the taxpayer keeps less of their hard earned income. Earned income is defined as that income that flows into our household as a result of having performed personal services. Thus, if we derive income solely from investments, chances are we would not be eligible to participate in a Keogh plan.

Furthermore, earned income is defined as net earnings from self-employment in which personal services we have rendered are responsible for the income produced. Capital is not relevant to this definition. The amount we can contribute is calculated by taking our gross business income and subtracting all business expenses. Reduce this amount by the contribution made to the Keogh plan and the result is our earned income from the business. Our annual contribution to any one account is the lesser of 20 percent of net earnings or $30,000. A profit-sharing Keogh is restricted to an annual contribution of the lesser of 15 percent of net earnings or $30,000.

If we have employees in our sole-proprietorship or partnership, we must include them under the same eligibility rules for participation and vesting that apply to corporate qualified plans (one-year of service and age 21).

We can make a contribution to our Keogh plan at any time during the taxable year and claim a deduction for that year. Furthermore, we can make a contribution after the close of the taxable year and deduct the amount so contributed to the prior taxable year. All we have to do is make our contribution for the preceding taxable year by the date due (including extensions) for filing the income tax return for that year (generally April 15th). It's necessary that our Keogh plan be in existence during the taxable year for which we are claiming our deduction (generally by December 31st). This procedure is different from the IRA requirements in that we can establish a trust and contribute up to April 15th and claim a deduction from our income for the preceding taxable year. Do not get the two programs confused, for to do so could be very costly to you.

We can participate in a qualified plan as a self-employed person, even though we work as an employee for another employer. Assume that you work for ABC Corporation, and in the evenings and weekends you maintain an office in which you practice as a bookkeeper. In such a case, you may participate in a qualified plan as a self-employed person with respect to your self-employed earnings, even though your employer maintains a qualified plan under which you are covered and participate as an employee. Your strategy should be to acquire all the tax deductions and tax deferral of earnings that you can possibly obtain.

If we own an unincorporated business, make a profit, and pay taxes, then we should consider this income replacement delivery system as a vehicle for accumulating money for retirement purposes. On the other hand, be aware that Keogh plans are denied certain exemptions from the prohibited transaction rules in connection with transactions in which the plan directly or indirectly:

- Lends any plan assets
- Pays any compensation for services rendered to the plan
- Buys any property for the plan from, or
- Sells any property to an owner-employee, a member of the family, or a corporation in which he or she owns, directly or indirectly, 50 percent or more of the total voting power of stock, or 50 percent or more of the dollar value of the stock.

The owner-employee cannot borrow from the plan. This limitation leads some sole-proprietors and partners to incorporate.

Tax Shelter Annuities (TSAs—403[B])

If we are an employee of a public school or certain tax-exempt and educational institutions, including churches, we are probably eligible to participate in a 403(b) plan. This means that the pension plan is set up under Section 403(b) of the Internal Revenue Code (IRC). This type of plan is also referred to as a **tax-deferred annuity** (TDA) or a **tax-shelter annuity** (TSA). A 403(b) plan permits contributions to be made that are deferred from current taxation. Our elective contributions cannot exceed $9,500 per year. If we contribute to another pension arrangement, such as a salary reduction plan under *Section 401(k)* of the Internal Revenue Code, or a simplified employee plan (SEP) under *Section 408*, or a government elective program under *Section 457*, the amount we can defer to our 403(b) plan is reduced by the amount contributed to the other plans. Under the *Tax Reform Act of 1986*, the contributory limitation to an elective 403(b) plan is higher than that imposed on elective 401(k) plans, or governmental elective plan under a 457 deferred compensation plan (DCP). Therefore, we may elect to defer our deductible contribution entirely into the 403(b) plan.

If we are now participating, or will participate in a 403(b) plan, we should be aware that the $9,500 limit placed on our elective annual contribution can be increased up to $12,500 provided certain requirements are met:

1. We have worked for our employer for 15 years.
2. The amount of the special increase over $9,500 cannot exceed $15,000 over our lifetime. Therefore, after five years of $12,500,

our elective annual contribution is reduced back to $9,500 (5 years x $3,000 = $15,000).
3. Our employer must be an educational organization, a hospital, church, or other tax-exempt organization structured under *Section 501 (c) (3)* of the Internal Revenue Code, and
4. The dollar amount in excess of $5,000 times years of service with the employer, less other deferrals made by our employer under 403(b), 401(k), or 457, exceeds $3,000.

Sounds like we have ventured into murky water, especially items 2 and 4. We have! We need to make an appointment to see the individual who administers employee benefit programs for our institution. Ask him or her how much you can contribute to your 403(b) plan and ask about the exclusion allowance and how it might apply to your specific situation. They will be glad to assist you, and over a period of time the water will become clear for you. Keep reading and asking questions until you are not only comfortable that you understand, but that you understand *Section 403(b)* well enough to explain it to your spouse and fellow workers. If you are planning to retire within the next ten years, contact your plan administrator today.

Deferred Compensation Plans (DCP) for State and Local Governmental Employees

The Internal Revenue Code has a special section titled "Section 457" that enables employees of state or local governmental agencies to participate in an elective deferred compensation arrangement. The *Tax Reform Act of 1986*, effective January 1, 1987, extended the provision of *Section 457* IRC to include tax-exempt organizations.

Under this type of arrangement, if we are eligible to participate, the amounts of compensation that we decide to defer, on a personal elective basis, are not taxed to us as current income, but are taxed as ordinary income when received. Furthermore, interest earnings are allowed to accumulate on a tax-deferred basis. A good deal? You bet, and it's a program that we should be participating in if we qualify. This program is an outstanding retirement delivery system with the following characteristics:

• A disciplined savings program, since our elective contributions are made through payroll deductions.

- Immediate federal and state tax reduction is realized with each payroll deduction.
- Interest earnings are allowed to accumulate on a tax deferred basis.
- We are not required to withdraw our contributions and earnings until we have attained age 70 1/2. This feature can assist us in providing some additional protection against inflation during our retirement years by providing for a substantial source of income to commence at age 70 1/2.

Every statutory program has requirements, and IRC *Section 457* is no different. Some of the key requirements are:

1. This is a big one! The amounts that we elect to defer and earnings on these amounts remain the property of our employer and are therefore subject to the claims of our employer's general creditors.
2. The maximum amount we can defer is the lesser of 25 percent of our gross earning (before salary reduction) or $7,500.
3. Any amounts being deferred under IRC *Section 403(b)* or IRC *Section 401(k)* must be taken into account in determining whether the overall $7,500 limit has been exceeded.
4. We must enter into a written deferred compensation agreement with our employer prior to the beginning of the pay period involved. This is normally accomplished once per year.
5. Once we've entered into a salary deferral arrangement, our funds can only be made available upon termination of service (employment). An unforeseeable emergency can be reason for our deferred compensation committee to authorize a withdrawal without termination of service.
6. This program provides for a total contribution and deduction of $15,000 per year for each of the three years preceding normal retirement under our plan. This is another big one! Don't let it pass you by. At this cycle of your life, your family is probably raised, your earnings are the highest they've ever been, and you have some interest income flowing into your household. You don't want to miss this $15,000 deduction opportunity if you are eligible. Go to your personnel office to see when and if this provision would apply to you. Enroll when eligible!

A deferred compensation plan under *Section 457* of the IRC is an excellent delivery program for retirement planning. It is not a Christmas Club, nor should you attempt to use it in that manner. This DCP is a serious, long-term retirement income supplemental program that gets the job done if you are eligible and elect to participate.

Social Security

This is a mandatory federal statutory retirement delivery system to which all working Americans contribute during their entire working careers. Social Security is a pay-as-you-go income replacement program, which means that there is no accumulation of funds in an irrevocable trust or through a contract with an insurance company. We are completely dependent on the ability of the federal government to tax its citizens in order to raise sufficient capital to pay the amount of money that we have been promised, at the age we were promised to receive such income. Will Social Security be there when we are ready to retire? Probably. Today, Social Security is a major political, economic, and social football in the United States. Congress is not likely to allow Social Security to either run out of money or disappear. Politicians will manipulate the program by increasing taxes, reducing cost of living allowances, and/or extending and changing eligibility requirements necessary to receive benefits, but the program will be there. What form it may take in the future is another question and issue. The political, economic, and social environment does change, and with these changes, programs come and go and others receive severe alterations.

When Congress adopted the *Social Security Act* in 1935, its fundamental purpose was to provide retirement benefits for wage earners. Today, the Social Security system provides a monthly cash flow for wage earners as well as to their spouses and dependents. Furthermore, Medicare was thrown into the package in 1965 to provide coverage for the cost of hospital stays and other required medical care once we attained age 65. These additions cost big dollars.

To get Social Security retirement payments for ourselves and our family, we must pay a "premium," collected as a payroll tax during our working years. Our contributions are matched by our employer "dollar-for-dollar."

Eligibility

The year is divided into four calendar quarters, and we receive Social Security credit for one or more of these quarters in a year (not more than four). For years before 1978, we receive one quarter of coverage for each quarter in which our earnings are $50 or more. For years after 1977, the amounts of earnings needed for one quarter of coverage has changed each year. In 1978, we needed total earnings of at least $250 per quarter; in 1987, we needed $460 of earnings per quarter to receive credit for an "includible" quarter of eligibility for Social Security benefits.

The number of credits we will need in order to receive benefits after we reach age sixty-two, or die, or become disabled, depends upon the date of our birth. No one is fully insured with credits less than a minimum of six quarters (1 1/2 years) of work and no one needs more than 40 quarters (10 years) of work.

If we attain retirement age and retire after 1990, we will need 40 quarters of coverage. These credits can be earned at any time after 1936 for workers, and after 1950 for the self-employed. There is no age limit on earning credit status to qualify for benefits.

Keep in mind that having a fully insured status means only that we are eligible for benefits. It does not mean that we qualify for maximum benefits. The amount of monthly payments that we will receive depends upon our average earnings. The more regularly we work under Social Security, and the higher our earnings, the higher our benefits.

Spouses

If we and our spouse are each entitled to benefits because of our own respective earnings, we will receive benefits independently of each other. However, a spouse who is a full-time homemaker is entitled to receive one-half of our benefits as long as we live or 75 percent of our benefits after we die. Furthermore, a surviving spouse is entitled to survivor benefits if he or she is age 60 or older (age 50 or older if our spouse is disabled). Our surviving children are entitled to benefits, too, if they are under age 18.

Disability

If we become disabled before age 65, we may qualify for monthly disability benefits. Certain members of our family may also be paid monthly benefits.

For us to be considered disabled under the Social Security law, we must have a condition so severe that it makes us unable to "engage in any substantial gainful activity," and is expected to last at least 12 months or is expected to result in death.

Disability Qualification

We generally must have Social Security credit for at least five years of work in a ten-year period preceding the disability.

Events that Stop Benefits

- Payments to a person receiving Social Security benefits of any kind are ended at the death of the person.
- Payments to a dependent spouse are ended if a divorce is granted.
- Payments to a survivor, relative, or dependent are lost if the person receiving them becomes entitled to benefits earned in his or her own right that are greater than the amount received as a dependent or survivor.
- Payments to a disabled person will stop if he or she is no longer disabled.
- Payments to a child will stop if that person marries.
- Payments to a wife under age 62 or widow or widower under age 62 will stop when that person no longer has in their care a child who is also entitled to monthly benefits.

Application for Benefits

Certain proofs must be supplied with our application for benefits. These are:

1. Proof of age. A birth certificate or a baptismal certificate or a hospital birth record are legal proof.

2. Proof of marriage must be filed with a claim by a husband, wife, widow, or widower.
3. Proof of death is needed in claims for survivor's benefits.
4. Proof of disability is required from our doctor or from a hospital or clinic where we have had treatment.
5. Proof of burial expense may be necessary for lump-sum death payments.

Do not delay in applying for Social Security benefits because you do not have some of the papers. Your local Social Security office will suggest other proofs that may be used.

Social Security Earnings History

Use form SSA-7004PC (Request for Statement of Earnings) available from your local Social Security Administration Office or post office to audit your earnings history (Figures 6.1 and 6.2). Even if you are years away from retirement, you should confirm your earnings history with the Social Security Administration every three to four years.

If you discover that some of your earnings aren't credited to you, you should contact your local Social Security office at once. Do not **delay**!

One closing thought applicable to Social Security: a reasonable person should not depend on any pay-as-you-go retirement system. To rely on such a system is to build our house at the edge of a cliff, facing the ocean. Certainly, some generation is going to be disappointed when the inevitable occurs.

Nonqualified Deferred Compensation Agreements

We have intentionally not included a section on this subject, since these plans are, for the most part, aimed at providing retirement income to key executives of an employer. This book has not been written with highly compensated executives as the primary subject. Nonqualified deferred compensation agreements are individually tailored between the employer and executive employee. The agreement may be as simple or as complex as the parties decide to make it.

Figure 6.1

You may request a statement of earnings from the Social Security Administration by submitting Form SSA-7004PC, available from any Social Security Administration office.

Social Security Administration
Wilkes-Barre Data Operations Center
P.O. Box 20
Wilkes-Barre, Pennsylvania 18703

(Sample)

	FOR SSA USE ONLY	
REQUEST FOR STATEMENT OF EARNINGS (PLEASE PRINT IN INK OR USE TYPEWRITER)	AX	●
	SP	●

I REQUEST A SUMMARY STATEMENT OF EARNINGS FROM MY SOCIAL SECURITY RECORD

NH — Full name you use in work or business / First / M.I. / Last ●

SN — Social Security number shown on your card ● DB | Your date of birth — Month / Day / Year A ●

MA — Other Social Security number(s) you have used ● SX | Your sex — ☐ Male ☐ Female ●

AK — Other name(s) you have used (Include your maiden name)

Figure 6.2

(Sample - Cont.)

PRIVACY STATEMENT

The Social Security Administration (SSA) is authorized to colect information asked on this form under section 205 of Social Security Act. It is needed so SSA can quickly identify your record and prepare the earnings statement you requested While you are not required to furnish the information, failure to do so may prevent your request from being processed. the information will be used primarily for issuing your earnings statement.

I am the individual to whom the record pertains. I understand that if I knowingly and willingly request or receive a record about an individual under false pretenses I would be guilty of a Federal crime and could be fined up to $5,000.

| Sign your name here: (Do not print) | Telephone No. (Area Code) | Date |

SEND THE STATEMENT TO: (to be completed in ALL cases.)

| PN | Name |

| AD | Address (Number and Street, Apt. No., P.O. Box, or Rural Route) |
| | City and State | ZP | Zip Code |

Form SSA-7004-PC-OPI (9/85)

Your Social Security Earnings Record

For a free statement of earnings credited to your Social Security record, complete this form. Use form for only one person.

All covered wages and self-employment income are reported under your name and Social Security number. So show your name and number exactly as onyour card. If you ever used another name or number, show this too.

The name and address blocks must be completed in order to receive a statement of your earnings.

If you have a separate question about Social Security, or want to discuss your statement when you get it, the people at any Social Security office will be glad to help you.

Chapter 7

Taxation of Lump-Sum Distributions

When we receive a check from the trustee of our qualified retirement plan, that check may well represent the largest single sum of money that we will ever see or have at one time. Since our working days may have ended with this check, it's important that we pay the least possible tax on the distribution. After all, the after-tax balance of these funds may have to last us (and our spouse) for the balance of our lives. Mistakes made at this juncture are hard to remedy.

The dramatic increase in dual income families in the United States, coupled with the enormous growth of Salary Reduction plans (401[k]), has resulted in large sums of money being held in trust for a very large employee base. Those employees will be extracting substantial amounts in the form of lump-sum distributions, now and in the future. But Congress wants more of this growing mountain of money than they have received in the past, and in order to accomplish this end, they have simply changed the ground rules for taxation of retirement money when distributed in the form of a lump-sum.

The *Tax Reform Act of 1986* substantially changed the tax treatment of **lump-sum distributions** (LSD) from qualified plans. These changes generally result in broadening the tax base, which simply means that most Americans will pay more taxes on lump-sum distributions from qualified plans.

The new law substitutes five-year forward income averaging for ten-year forward income averaging, both very advantageous tax methods. The law restricts five-year forward income averaging by providing that we can elect such averaging only after we attain age 59 1/2 and receive a lump-sum distribution. At this moment in time, we must either roll it over to an Individual Retirement Account (IRA), another qualified retirement plan, or subject the distribution to ordinary income taxation, which may not be a wise choice.

Age 50 or Older—January 1, 1986

Generally, here's how an LSD works: if we were age 50 or older on January 1, 1986, we are eligible to use the ten-year forward income averaging method. If we elect to use the ten-year forward income averaging method, our tax is computed by using the 1986 tax rates for a single individual. In addition, we can elect the long-term capital gain method for that portion of the distribution that is attributable to our participation in the plan before January 1, 1974. The capital gain portion is taxed at a 20 percent rate. If we take advantage of this election, we may also elect the new five-year forward income averaging treatment for the portion of the distribution attributable to the period after January 1, 1974, without regard to the new after-age-59 1/2 restriction.

Under Age 50—January 1, 1986

If we were under age 50 on January 1, 1986, and receive a lump-sum distribution from a qualified plan, we are entitled to calculate our taxes using the five-year forward income averaging method, once in our lifetime, and only if we receive the funds after attaining age 59 1/2.

With these factors in mind, our payment from a qualified retirement plan may be eligible to receive this special tax treatment only if the distribution meets all of the following circumstances:

1. It was from a qualified retirement plan.
2. It was from all of the employer's qualified plans of one kind. "One kind" means pension, profit-sharing, or stock bonus.

3. It was for the entire amount due us.
4. It was paid within a single tax-year. This is our tax-year, which for most of us is January 1st to December 31st.
5. It was paid for any one of these reasons:
   a. our death
   b. we attain age 59 1/2 or older at the time of the distribution
   c. we quit, retired, were laid off, or were fired.

After these specifications have been met, we must complete Form 4972, titled "Tax on Lump-Sum Distributions," and attach the completed form to our Form 1040 (See Figure 7.1 for sample Form 4972). Form 4972 taxes this money without regard to any of our other income or deductions.

The employer, the fiduciary of the trust, or whoever actually pays the distribution is required to provide us with certain information on Form 1099R. The information to be furnished is:

- The total amount distributed
- The total taxable amount of the distribution
- The ordinary income portion and the capital gain portion of the distribution
- The amount contributed by the employee
- The net unrealized appreciation on any securities of the employer corporation

If we qualify for both the five-year and ten-year forward averaging, do not assume that the ten-year forward averaging will result in a lower tax. Remember, the ten-year forward averaging method will always use the 1986 single taxpayer rate table. The five-year forward income averaging uses current rates. We should compute our tax under both methods in order to be sure as to the lowest possible tax that we need to pay.

Most accountants and tax attorneys have access to services that will provide printouts reflecting every possible option available to us when we receive a lump-sum distribution. Spend a few dollars to consult with an accountant and tax attorney. The time and money we spend may save us thousands of dollars, not to mention the avoidance of potential grief.

Avoid going to an accountant or attorney without having done your own research on this topic. Become familiar with the terms and understand generally how a lump-sum distribution is calculated. Get a

Figure 7.1

Form **4972**	**Tax on Lump-Sum Distributions** (Use This Form Only for Lump-Sum Distributions From Qualified Retirement Plans)	OMB No. 1545-0193
Department of the Treasury Internal Revenue Service	▶ **Attach to Form 1040 or Form 1041.** ▶ **See separate instructions.**	19**91** Attachment Sequence No. **28**
Name of recipient of distribution		Identifying number

Part I   Complete this part to see if you qualify to use Form 4972.

			Yes	No
1	Did you roll over any part of the distribution? If "Yes," do not complete the rest of this form.	1		
2	Was the retirement plan participant born before 1936 (and, if deceased, was the participant at least 50 years old at the date of death)? If "No," do not complete the rest of this form	2		
3	Was this a lump-sum distribution from a qualified pension, profit-sharing, or stock bonus plan? (See **Distributions That Qualify for the 20% Capital Gain Election or for 5- or 10-Year Averaging** in the instructions.) If "No," do not complete the rest of this form.	3		
4	Was the participant in the plan for at least 5 years before the year of the distribution?	4		
5	Was this distribution paid to you as a beneficiary of a plan participant who died? If you answered "No" to 4 **and** 5, do not complete the rest of this form.	5		
6	Was the plan participant:			
a	An employee who received the distribution because he or she quit, retired, was laid off or fired?	6a		
b	Self-employed or an owner-employee who became permanently and totally disabled before the distribution?	6b		
c	Age 59½ or older at the time of the distribution? If you answered "No" to question 5 and **all** parts of question 6, do not complete the rest of this form.	6c		
7	Did you use Form 4972 for any distribution received after 1986 from a plan for the same plan participant, including you, for whom the 1991 distribution was made? If "Yes," do not complete the rest of this form	7		

If you qualify to use this form, you may choose to use Part II, Part III, or Part IV; **or** Part II and Part III; **or** Part II and Part IV.

Part II   Complete this part to choose the 20% capital gain election. (See instructions.)

1	Capital gain part from Box 3 of Form 1099-R. (See instructions.)	1	
2	Multiply line 1 by 20% (.20) and enter here. If you do not elect to use Part III or Part IV, also enter the amount on Form 1040, line 39, or Form 1041, Schedule G, line 1b.	2	

Part III   Complete this part to choose the 5-year averaging method. (See instructions.)

1	Ordinary income from Form 1099-R, Box 2a minus Box 3. If you did not make the Schedule D election or complete Part II, enter the taxable amount from Box 2a of Form 1099-R. (See instructions.)	1	
2	Death benefit exclusion. (See instructions.)	2	
3	Total taxable amount—Subtract line 2 from line 1	3	
4	Current actuarial value of annuity, if applicable (from Form 1099-R, Box 8)	4	
5	Adjusted total taxable amount—Add lines 3 and 4. If this amount is $70,000 or more, skip lines 6 through 9, and enter this amount on line 10	5	
6	Multiply line 5 by 50% (.50), but **do not** enter more than $10,000.	6	
7	Subtract $20,000 from line 5. If line 5 is $20,000 or less, enter -0-	7	
8	Multiply line 7 by 20% (.20)	8	
9	Minimum distribution allowance—Subtract line 8 from line 6	9	
10	Subtract line 9 from line 5	10	
11	Federal estate tax attributable to lump-sum distribution. Do not deduct on Form 1040 or Form 1041 the amount attributable to the ordinary income entered on line 1. (See instructions.)	11	
12	Subtract line 11 from line 10	12	
13	Multiply line 12 by 20% (.20)	13	
14	Tax on amount on line 13. See instructions for Tax Rate Schedule	14	
15	Multiply line 14 by five (5). If no entry on line 4, skip lines 16 through 21. Enter the amount on line 22	15	
16	Divide line 4 by line 5 and enter the result as a decimal. (See instructions.)	16	
17	Multiply line 9 by the decimal amount on line 16	17	
18	Subtract line 17 from line 4	18	
19	Multiply line 18 by 20% (.20)	19	
20	Tax on amount on line 19. See instructions for Tax Rate Schedule	20	
21	Multiply line 20 by five (5)	21	
22	Subtract line 21 from line 15. (Multiple recipients, see instructions.)	22	
23	Tax on lump-sum distribution—Add Part II, line 2, and Part III, line 22. Enter on Form 1040, line 39, or Form 1041, Schedule G, line 1b. ▶	23	

For Paperwork Reduction Act Notice, see separate instructions.   Cat. No. 13187U   Form **4972** (1991) copy of Form 4972 from your local IRS office and review the form before your appointment. The form is generally self-explanatory. Go to your local library. The staff will be able to assist you in finding "lay" person's material explaining taxes on lump-sum distributions. See what written tax advice your company may provide. Read it, realize it is complex, and seek competent assistance. Get involved and stay involved. Don't assume that anyone is automatically going to do what is in your best interest. Investigate all options that are available to you, then select the option that is best for you.

The IRA Rollover: The Lump-Sum Alternative at Retirement

The IRA rollover can be an effective way for us to gain control of our assets, taxes, and long-term security needs, and at the same time maintain control of our assets in a trust or custodial account. We need to understand how this retirement delivery system can work for us.

The requirements for an Individual Retirement Account are set forth in *Section 408* of the Internal Revenue Code (IRC). The "account" is actually a trust organized in the United States for the exclusive benefit of an individual or his or her beneficiaries. The Trustee is normally a commercial bank or in the case of a custodial account, a commercial insurance company.

The important advantage of the **IRA rollover account**, compared to the other distribution options, results from the fact that our retirement funds remain in trust. Our dollars remain unattached—unattached in that these funds cannot be taken or held as security for a judgement. The trust is a legal entity, apart from our assets. The trust status of the IRA helps to insure that the retirement funds will actually be available at retirement. Thus, if we are forced to file for bankruptcy or become liable for a law suit, our money will be shielded from creditors. The funds in a qualified retirement account are only available to us. This protected status can be an attractive advantage if we are sorting our options for lump-sum distributions. Of course, there are potential disadvantages that must be considered. For example, if we were 50 years old before January 1, 1986, and the lump-sum distribution is from a corporate retirement plan, the distribution may be entitled to the favorable ten-year forward tax averaging rules. If rolled into an IRA, however, these funds are automatically taxed as ordinary income during the year(s) we receive the funds.

Another disadvantage stems from the distribution restrictions on the IRA. We may not receive distributions from the trust before reaching age 59 1/2 without also incurring a 10 percent nondeductible tax penalty on the distribution. The 10 percent penalty tax will not apply to the following distributions:

- Death
- Becoming disabled
- Distributions made in a series of substantial equal periodic payments made for our life or the joint lives of ourself and our beneficiaries
- After we attain age 55 and have separated from service on account of early retirement under the plan
- On account of medical expenses in excess of 7 1/2 percent of AGI, and
- Divorce order

Furthermore, we may not borrow or pledge IRA funds. Similarly, we must begin receiving payments from our IRA by April 1st the year following the year in which we turn 70 1/2, regardless of whether we remain employed.

For example, if we attained age 70 1/2 in 1992, we must start receiving funds from our IRA account no later than April 1, 1993. Failure to comply can result in severe, nondeductible tax penalties. It is important for us to understand when an IRA rollover may be used. The requirements for a rollover contribution are set forth in *Section 408(d)(3)* of the IRC. In general, a distribution from a qualified plan may be rolled over, tax deferred, to an IRA if it qualifies as a lump-sum distribution. The qualified plan may be a corporate pension or profit-sharing plan, including a salary reduction plan under *Section 401(k)*, a Keogh or HR-10 plan, a Tax Shelter Annuity (TSA) under *Section 403(b)*, or even another IRA. A payout qualifies as a lump-sum distribution if the entire balance credited to our account is paid within one tax year. The lump-sum distribution may be the result of our separation from service; reaching age 59 1/2; or a plan termination by the employer. In the event of our death, the IRA is also available to our spouse.

Be careful to watch for this. A deferred compensation plan established by a governmental tax-exempt employer, under *Section 457*, can **never** be rolled into an IRA. Nor can any other nonqualified deferred compensation plan be rolled into an IRA.

No matter what the sources of the rollover, the payout must be transferred into an IRA within 60 days after the receipt of the final payment. We are not required to transfer the entire amount into an IRA. We may keep part of the distribution to spend as we choose, but the portion not rolled over is taxed as ordinary income in the year received. Further, if we are not 59 1/2 the 10 percent penalty tax may apply.

Educators should be careful if they are participating in Teachers Insurance Annuity Association/College Retirement Equity Fund (TIAA/CREF), and are withdrawing funds from the Supplemental Retirement Account (SRA). You may not rollover your balance into an IRA account, unless the SRA account balance represents at least 50 percent of the total balance of all TIAA/CREF accounts you own.

No special tax treatment applies to the portion of the distribution that is not deposited in the IRA rollover account. Your contributions to a retirement plan, using after-tax dollars, cannot be rolled over under any circumstances. These after-tax contributions form a cost basis and must be extracted from the lump-sum distribution prior to the rollover being completed. Interest earned on our after-tax contributions may be rolled over. This is handled in this manner, since we have never paid taxes on the accumulation of earnings. Continued tax-deferral of interest earnings is acceptable.

A rollover distribution from a retirement plan provides three distinct advantages:

1. Postponement of tax payments.
2. Possible reduction of tax liability on the eventual payout, and
3. Continued tax-deferred buildup of retirement savings in a trust account.

Item (3) may be the most valuable hedge against inflation; that is, the tax-deferred buildup of our money until April 1st of the year following our attaining age 70 1/2. This strategy will enable us to give ourselves a nice raise at age 70 1/2.

Thousands of people in our society are growing poorer as a result of inflation. But the most common reason for poverty in America among the aged is lack of planning for the future. Don't let this happen to you. The most ambitious public or private retirement programs will never provide the kind of retirement we deserve. If we plan to live above subsistence level, there is no escape from providing for ourselves, and the sooner we begin the easier it will be. Time value of money is the answer.

Keep in mind that legislation changes frequently. Therefore, we encourage you to go to your local library to get the latest information regarding IRA rollovers. IRA rollover information written in nonlegal terms is available. This chapter is intended to provide you with a general foundation and to point you into the right direction.

The accountant, pension consultant, or tax attorney can all assist us in the selection process, but the final decision must rest with each of us. Carefully evaluate your options. We must live the rest of our lives with our decision, not the accountant, pension consultant, or tax attorney.

Now, what does the future hold for taxation of lump-sum distributions? In the name of pension policy simplification, eventually Congress will no doubt cause this chapter to be obsolete. How? By simply taxing all funds received from defined benefit and defined contribution plans as ordinary income, regardless of the manner or condition in which funds are received. What will this mean to us, the taxpayer? It will mean that we will have less money for retirement living and Congress will have more of our money for spending and redistributing. The pursuit of dignity requires personal attention and commitment during all of our working years. See Figure 7.2 for accumulation amounts based on various interest rates for a lump-sum distribution from a corporate plan and from a TSA/TDA.

Figure 7.2

Corporate Retirement Plan Accumulation

Lump-Sum Distribution From a
Corporate Plan — $100,000

After	8%	10%	14%	16%
10 years	$ 215,890	$ 259,370	$ 370,722	$ 441,144
15 years	$ 317,220	$ 417,720	$ 713,794	$ 926,552
30 years	$1,006,270	$1,744,940	$5,095,016	$8,584,988

Tax-Shelter Annuity Accumulation

Lump-Sum Distribution From a
TSA/TDA — $25,000

After	8%	10%	14%	16%
10 years	$ 53,973	$ 64,843	$ 92,681	$ 110,286
15 years	$ 79,305	$ 104,430	$ 178,448	$ 231,638
30 years	$ 251,568	$ 436,235	$1,273,754	$2,146,247

Chapter 8

Preparing for Retirement

Learning to live in retirement, like anything else that is successful, requires the expenditure of positive energy. In business we have been efficiently indoctrinated concerning the utilization of scarce resources: time, people, material, and money. When we retire, these same scarce resources and the need to efficiently manage them does not go away. Instead of viewing scarce resources as an integral part of our business or professional life, we need to view scarce resources as also being an integral part of our retirement. And make no mistake about it, they are. It is important that we don't fool ourselves about retirement. A checklist telling us what we need to do and expect in preparation for and during retirement can be found in any library. The shelves are full of "checklist retirement books." We have no intentions of duplicating what has been previously done in abundance.

First, however, we would like to address some myths that are prevalent in many retirement books and in matters of economics, taxation, politics, social, family and health care needs.

If we open any book addressing the issue of retirement, we can find that we need approximately 70 percent of our preretirement income in order to live in a reasonable and dignified manner during our "golden years." The economics of retirement are changing thanks to inflation and taxation. At 5 percent annual rate of inflation, we lose 50 percent of the purchasing power of our money in 14+ years. If one retires at age 65, actuaries tell us we can anticipate another 16 to 20 years. Simple economics tell us that we should retire with an amount of monthly income in excess of our final pay. How much more? Probably about 30 percent more. This would mean a realistic target for initial retirement pay would be 130 percent of one's final pay, not 70 percent. Inflation will erode our purchasing power 50 percent in just 14 years, at an annual inflation rate of 5 percent. At the end of 14 years, we will be left with 65 percent of the level of preretirement income and find ourselves still alive. Each year that we live, our life expectancy increases. Furthermore, Congress will keep raising taxes on the elderly by paying less for Medicare coverage for both Parts A and B and implementing a "means test" for Social Security income and Medicare coverage eligibility. When Congress imposes such policies, the impact is the same as if we were taxed directly. Inflation is nothing more than a tax imposed on us by Congress, and it is a direct result of budgetary and policy formation by that legislative body.

We must start early in life to prepare for our later years and time value of money is a major component of the answer. We must be realistic. Medical expenses will continue to increase at a rate faster than inflation. Much of this "inflation" can be and will be attributed directly to the government's policy in paying Medicare and Medicaid claims. That policy is very simple: pay less and less of the actual cost of health care, thereby transferring the cost and responsibility to the individual and business. This is not a new game, but one that started in the 1970s, and the game will continue.

Recognize certain facts concerning retirement. These facts cannot be ignored:

1. We must have a plan for time utilization.
2. We must establish a wellness program for ourself, and if married, our spouse.
3. We need human support systems, not high technology support systems. In other words, we need each other.
4. We must take charge and be responsible for our financial management.
5. We are responsible for our personal fulfillment.

This business of "I'd be O.K. if only you would change" doesn't work anymore—if it ever did.

Many individuals are very confident that once retired, they can readily become a consultant with the freedom to set their own hours. This is a common belief by people with business titles and good business contacts. Once retired, the title goes as do the business contacts. The reality is that most retired consultants don't last long. They become expensive to the company hiring them; and contrary to popular conception, after a few months, it becomes clear that he/she is simply not needed. In the short term, the company may have a particular business problem and it wants to take advantage of the retiree's business contacts. But once this goal is accomplished, the retiree/consultant is, politely, out. Don't live in a fantasy world about all the great contributions you will render to society once retired. Once that job title is removed, we move in different circles. A chapter in our life is closed and a new chapter is clearly opened.

You may think this is not true in the civic affairs arena, but it is. Key positions, such as chairmanships and presidencies (the top offices), go to young people and almost invariably to people working with a job title. Their jobs give them influence and importance—they are automatically networked. We are not saying this is good or bad, fair or unfair, just or unjust. Again, it is just the way it *is*.

First Things First

If we are planning to retire in the near future, now is the time to make a list of all employers for whom we have ever worked. Send each employer a letter stating the dates of our employment and request forms claiming the retirement benefits that are due us. It is shocking the number of Americans who have vested benefits payable to them, but never file a claim. We don't want to be another statistic by not filing a claim. The cost to file a claim form is the time that we spend writing the letter, the price of the envelope, and a postage stamp. We might surprise ourselves with the results. Make that list of employers and send a letter today. (See sample letter, Figure 8.1.)

Send a letter even if you've already retired because you may have benefits waiting for you. Our previous employers have 30 days, by law, to respond to our request.

You may wonder how it is that an individual can have vested benefits due and payable at retirement, but never file a claim. Certainly, no reasonable person would retire without claiming what is legally theirs in the form of additional income replacement and health care coverage. Well, it is not uncommon and the answer is probably very

---

Figure 8.1   First Things First

Draft
Sample Letter
Requesting Income Replacement
and
Retiree Health Care Benefits

To: President
    XYZ Corporation (Company)
    Address

Re: Your Name
    Your Social Security Number
    Dates of Employment

Dear Sir:

I was employed by XYZ Corporation during the period of _____
to _____ 19___. My job while employed by XYZ Corporation was
_____.

I will soon be retiring (or I have retired) and request that you send me
your retirement package and necessary forms so I can claim my vested
benefits from XYZ Corporation.

Your attention to this matter is appreciated.

Sincerely,

Your Name
Your Address

---

simple: The individual never understood the benefit programs that his or her employer was providing in the first place. This lack of understanding is caused by educational and motivational deficits. Or, put another way, it is simply not wanting to assume responsibility for our own well-being. There is a prevailing attitude within the labor force of the United States at all levels—senior management, middle management, line supervisors and workers—that someone else will provide for our income replacement and health care needs, when needed. Therefore, we need not bother.

Retirement planning, whether for individuals, institutions, or corporations, involves two stages—the accumulation of dollars during our working years, and the payout of dollars in the form of income replacement payments and health care coverage during our retired years.

The three primary sources of income during retirement are Social Security, retirement plans, and personal savings.

No matter what the future holds for us, we need to save. Will Rogers once said, "I never met a man who was sorry he saved money." Had Will Rogers made this statement in today's environment, he probably would have said, "I never met a person who was sorry they saved money."

Our company pension plan and Social Security will not be enough. Defined benefit plans, employer pay all, with a predictable income replacement base are rapidly becoming a dying delivery system. Congress is legislating these programs out of existence. Defined benefit pension plans have simply become too expensive and time consuming for most employers to administer. The negatives of this delivery system have exceeded the positives. Defined contribution plans will dominate the future as the prime income replacement vehicle. What you see is what you get.

Investment risk, unlike the defined benefit plan where risk is retained by the employer, will be transferred to the individual participant. We, the participant, will be responsible to see that contributions accumulated are sufficient for us to achieve our financial objectives. We will have to stay informed and recognize that we alone are responsible to direct the investments of our retirement funds. Much of the fiduciary liability will be transferred to the individual plan participant.

In the future, employers will cut back on medical coverage for retirees due to cost. FASB *Statement 106* has pushed this issue to the forefront. *Statement 106* requires employers offering retiree health care coverage to carry the future cost as a liability on the corporate balance sheet. This requirement could drive the value of corporate stock down.

What does this all mean to the individual? It means that we need to be prepared to carry a greater financial burden for our health care and health services during our retirement years. We believe that we will see the day when a member of Congress will take the floor and state "The elderly in the United States are utilizing more health care and requiring more expensive procedures than any other segment of our population." Furthermore, "The elderly health care cost can no longer be passed to future generations—today, the elderly must 'bite the bullet.'" We can forget the many years we and our employers sent money to Congress for our future medical bills. There will be no money there. The year will probably be around 2000, if not sooner.

Cost of utilities, property taxes, and repairs will probably increase more than the rate of inflation. Certainly, our utilities bills will probably go up, not down, after retirement because we will be home more. Generally, homes may not appreciate in the 1990s as they did in the 1980s. Home equity annuities will become more popular in the future, as retired people find that they have not properly planned for the "golden years." There will be a significant movement by many financial institutions in marketing this type of "annuity." We would all do well to become familiar with this home equity vehicle in case we need it to finance a portion of our retirement years.

Money is important for retirement, but it is the lifestyle decisions that are really important. Money is important to the extent that it is needed to finance our lifestyle decisions. These decisions include where we will live, vacation, and spend our spare time. A comfortable and successful retirement is about fulfilling our objectives and not about accumulating money. We want to enjoy our lives to the fullest, which is a concept based on our individual definition of happiness. Money is the means to assist us in achieving our ends, but money is not an end in itself.

Part IV

Part IV

Chapter 9

Health Care in the United States: Cost, Quality, and Access

One shocking figure tells the story: American's expenditures for health care rose over *900 percent* between 1970 and 1991. Furthermore, no end is in sight. Government figures indicate that outlays for health care will rise from the $192 billion annual expenditure level of 1968 to more than $750 billion by 1992. Can we afford it? People want unlimited access to medical care despite the expenses; even those who preach stringent cost control will demand the very best when a family member becomes critically ill.

More people will continue to demand more services, despite spiraling health care costs, until someone protests, "Isn't 12.5 percent of our gross national product enough to spend on health care"? We must have limits. Because of our current climate of civil liability, the physician cannot set those limits. *Society* must set the goals and limits of administering health care.

In 1965, the United States government entered the health care field with Medicare and Medicaid. These payment programs set the standard of care and paid for health care for those covered. Now, 28 years later under the same systems, the government pays less than the actual cost of that care demanded. The financial obligations of political promises to Medicare and Medicaid recipients have been shifted to employers and private citizens.

Thus, for better or worse, those who pay the bills must set the limits in health care and costs. We must ensure that in our time of need, appropriate health care will be available to us. By deciding how much we are willing to pay, we will determine the allocation of resources in America that will define medicine for ourselves and for the next generation.

We suggest that the system be reformed on a sound, free enterprise basis in a way that preserves the quality and accessibility of the system. While this is perhaps the key issue in the continuing national debate over America's health care system, there are several related questions:

1. How much health care is enough? Many Americans confuse quality with quantity.
2. How much is the average person willing and able to pay for health care?
3. Does the system weaken cost controls when most Americans have insurance (third-party payment) to cover their medical bills?
4. Can the present system of health care delivery and payment be made more efficient?

There are several reasons for the rapid and continuing rise in hospital and health care costs, reasons that are either part of the system or are simply unavoidable. Some of these are:

1. Increasing outpatient treatment
2. Increasing labor costs
3. More expensive technology
4. New complex treatments
5. Rising malpractice insurance rates
6. Our aging population
7. Extension of benefits

We will explore each of these factors in turn.

Increasing Outpatient Treatment

Reducing cost by increasing the number of patients treated within the hospital allows all but the most ill patients to be cared for outside the hospital environment. This means that the patients remaining in the hospital for treatment will require more extensive and expensive care. With fewer admissions and increasing numbers of empty beds, there are fewer patients to share in the fixed expense of plant maintenance. In 31 states, bed occupancy is less than 50 percent. This drives up the cost per hospital patient.

The government and insurance companies felt that they could save money by moving lesser procedures away from the expensive hospital environment. The minor procedures, such as breast augmentation, hernia repair, and removal of hemorrhoids, were moved to the less expensive outpatient environment. Insurance companies encouraged the shift by paying 100 percent for outpatient procedures, but cut reimbursement to 80 percent if the same procedure was performed in the hospital. Outpatient care is also frequently more convenient and less time consuming.

Recent radio advertisements promoting the use of outpatient facilities have encouraged over-utilization. Ads promoting "Free transportation to and from the center on the day of surgery" and "Surgery this morning and home tonight" are common. When procedures are shifted from an inpatient to an outpatient environment, they are no longer subject to hospital quality assurance review. Basically unregulated, these outpatient procedures continue to increase. Rather than reducing expenses as proposed, the transfer has simply driven costs still higher. To pay generously in an unregulated environment results in increased cost.

Increasing Labor Cost

Inflation has returned to the health care labor market. With deteriorating workplace conditions in our hospitals, as hospitals cut staffing to become more efficient; as more and more critically ill AIDS victims require care; as the population ages; as only the more urgent cases are now treated as inpatients; as health care workers demand higher pay. Poor working conditions and burnout are causing nurses to move into other fields. As conditions in the health care industry become recognized, nursing school enrollment continues to drop. Eighty-seven percent of all hospitals now have unfilled RN positions. This demand for nurses has raised their salaries and benefits faster than the rise of inflation.

More Expensive Technology

The price of medical technology continues to rise. Fifteen years ago a physical examination might have included the use of a $50,000 x-ray machine. Ten years ago a patient could have undergone a CAT (computed axial tomography) scan, which provides far more information, but the machine would have cost between $500,000 and $1,000,000. Today, the same problem can be clinically assessed in remarkable detail by MRI (magnetic resonance imaging). Such equipment, however will cost from $1,500,000 to $4,000,000.

The new technology is a supplement rather than a replacement for earlier procedures. A physician doesn't order simply for screening purposes a test that costs a thousand dollars. He or she begins by requesting a standard x-ray. Any abnormalities discovered are then evaluated using CAT or MRI.

For example, a spot on the lungs discovered by a chest x-ray 20 years ago would routinely have been surgically removed. Today, a physician in such a situation would first obtain a CAT scan, which might reveal that the lesion was benign and there would be no need for surgery. On the other hand, if the scan indicated an inoperable lesion, a useless surgical procedure could be avoided.

Then shouldn't the new technology reduce costs by decreasing unnecessary surgery? Yes, but it also promotes surgical volumes because these machines reveal many lesions that are not visible on a standard x-ray. Furthermore, since a greater number of diseases are discovered and treated at earlier stages, more patients now enjoy extended life expectancies and eventually will place greater stress on the Medicare system.

New Complex Treatments

Extended complex treatments are now available for once fatal diseases. Lung cancer, for example, is the number one cancer killer in the United States. Its rate of occurrence is also increasing faster than any other form of cancer.

In 1991, 149,000 new cases and 135,000 deaths were reported, indicating that with conventional treatment the cure rate for this disease is dismal.

Under standard management, the five-year survival rate from Stage I lung cancer (the lowest grade) is 35 percent; from Stage II, 15 percent; and from Stage III (often considered incurable), much worse.

Fourteen years ago, some thoracic surgeons began working on an advanced management program to improve patients' survival. Today, surgeons who use these new techniques have improved the five-year survival rates dramatically. The cure rate for Stage I lung cancer has increased to 80 percent; for Stage II, 60 percent; and for Stage III (when confined to the chest), 30 percent. These patients have a higher cure rate and a long life expectancy, but they are also in the hospital longer.

Although the centers offering this new treatment can cure a significant number of previously inoperable patients, the costs of such care will be much greater than those for patients dying at home under conventional treatment. It is more expensive to care for a patient after a major surgical resection.

This cured patient will require close follow-up for early detection of possible recurrence. The patient may also live to have other unrelated illnesses that will further drain the system of scarce and needed resources.

Rising Malpractice Insurance Rates

Malpractice rates have driven costs even higher. Many cardiothoracic surgeons pay $100,000 to $150,000 each year for malpractice coverage. In many states, adequate coverage is not available at any price. Even so, these inflated rates offer only limited coverage, and the high cost of such liability premiums must be passed on to the patient.

Our Aging Population

The aging population brings us face to face with a higher incidence of cancer, heart disease, and stroke. As care of the elderly and debilitated becomes centered about the nursing home rather than the family unit, the costs for their treatment increases proportionately.

Extension of Benefits

Health care plans now cover treatments such as organ transplantation, premature infant care, and psychiatric care. In each of these categories a single patient can accumulate bills of $100,000 to $500,000.

Just a few years ago, the physician of a patient with kidney failure could only explain to the patient and his family how organ failure progressed and how they could provide for the most comfortable death for their family members. Today, dialysis is available to all Americans at a national cost of over $2 billion dollars.

Though this figure may seem prohibitive, it is but a fraction of the price of universal access to complex organ replacement. Certain medical emergencies can also make heavy demands upon insurance funds and the cost of care for an ill premature infant may be $250,000. Furthermore, treatment for a single schizophrenic patient can cost as much as $400,000.

There are approximately three people paying into Medicare for each Medicare recipient. Do we need a list of services to be paid with available funds? What will our Medicare bills be tomorrow if we continue to expand coverage to new categories of illness? We could conceal costs temporarily simply by draining the Social Security Retirement Fund to meet the Medicare shortfall, though such political expediency is surely less appealing to the retiree.

The Rising Health Care Premium

It is important to distinguish health care premiums from the costs of health care. While costs have risen at about 7 percent per year, premiums have increased disproportionately. Consider the newspaper headlines from the *New York Times* of January 12, 1988: (insurance rates) "stun employees and workers," "Premiums rise 10 to 70 percent," "Medicare up by 38.5 percent."

Let's look at these disparities. For several years, premiums have increased less than the cost of care. During this time, Health Maintenance Organizations (HMOs), which had been established to help control health care costs, often were subsidized by the government, thus enabling them to charge less than the cost of the care they provided. This gave them a share of the market and forced competing carriers to keep health care premiums low.

The bull stock market of the 1980s enabled insurance companies to earn more on their investments. The "bull market" slowed down. Costs rose. Insurance companies earned less on their funds. Government subsidies to HMOs ceased. Health care premiums were increased sharply so that provider institutions could make a profit and continue to exist. Premiums cannot remain lower than costs indefinitely in a free enterprise society. Many cash-strapped providers increased their charges to make up for previous losses. Health care charges are increasing much more than the cost of health care.

Quality in Medicine

Most people in our society view health care as a right. Quality health care is viewed as a system that can fulfill their needs at any given time whether that be routine evaluation, emergency treatment, long-term care, education, or counseling. Satisfaction with the system will depend upon three factors:

1. The patient's choice of physicians
2. The vehicle by which health care is delivered
3. Outside forces (e.g., legislation or the liability crisis) that affect access to a service or physician.

Choice of physician is the preeminent determinant of satisfaction. Certainly, the physician with competence and integrity will deliver the best medical care at the lowest cost in any system. Even so, price is not a reliable yardstick. There may be wide variations in charges for the same procedure. High fees may reflect greed, not quality, and low fees might be the highest of all if more procedures are performed.

How then to choose a physician? Begin with an interview. Does your physician relate well to you? Do your questions make your doctor insecure? Should such a person make life-and-death decisions concerning you? What is their educational background? Where did they receive their undergraduate degree and their internship/residency training? Are they certified by the appropriate American Board? How much experience have they had with problems like yours? If they are a surgeon, what is their mortality rate? Whom do the physicians in your community consult when they have a problem in a particular field? "Outcome analysis" is important for a large corporation selecting a medical team.

When making your selection, remember the other side of the coin. An incompetent physician has less understanding than a more capable one. A physician may continue to spend your money on tests but never establish a diagnosis; or worse, they may make the wrong diagnosis. Countless Americans have died of massive heart attacks because their cardiac pain was misinterpreted as gallbladder disease.

Even if a medical problem is defined, the incompetent physician, by their very inability, may further aggravate the condition. Twenty percent of all hospital deaths in the United States are thought to be "iatrogenic" (related to the doctor's treatment). Death by medicine is not attractive or inexpensive. Inept physicians should be avoided.

The Difficulties of Health Care Cost Analysis

When we consider the increasing spiral of health care costs, we must separate the statistics of sensational journalism from the facts. A *Wall Street Journal* article stated that in 1986 medical costs rose ten times faster than inflation. The consumer price index rose 1.9 percent. Hospital costs increased 19 percent. This data was based on a study by Equicor/Hospital Corporation of America. It involved 1,863 hospitals. In actuality, there are more than 6,000 hospitals in our country. American hospitalization data based on all United States hospitals showed an increase not of 19 percent but of 8.4 percent. Over the past six years, medical care costs have risen about 7 percent per year, or 2 percent above an assumed annual inflation rate of 5 percent. Certainly, health care costs are rising, but perhaps not to the extent reflected in some of our more sensational lay press articles.

As a further complication, health care costs in our society have not been determined by the basic economic laws of **supply and demand**, the price competition basic to our industries. **Demand** is the price a consumer is willing to pay for a service or product. **Supply** is the amount of service or product a manufacturer is willing to provide for sale at each price level. As prices rise in the industrial marketplace, demand falls and as prices are reduced, demand increases.

This was not true of the health care system. Since health care providers used to deliver health care in a noncompetitive environment and since patients or other buyers used not to compete with one another, hospitals and doctors have shuffled costs and charges from patient to patient depending on economic circumstances.

Each time Congress capped Medicare payments to hospitals, the costs were shifted to the states and other customers. As states limited their Medicaid hospital payments, the private sector had to make up the difference. When Congress restricted payments on certain medical procedures performed in hospitals, doctors undertook these same procedures in their offices or clinics. Today, this practice of cost shifting from public to private sector can no longer be hidden, and the burden to the individuals and employers is enormous.

Now employers and health care plans are fighting back. They are making financially strained hospitals bid for blocks of patients. Hospitals that were previously shielded from market pressures are quickly shedding middle management and extraneous personnel to let them become more economical. Hospitals unsuccessful in their bids to health care insurers are going out of business. As in private industry, the expectation of secure lifetime employment is gone from the health care field. For the community, hospital survival is now victory.

Access

Access to health care in our country is an entirely different problem. To the patient with standard fee-for-service health insurance who can afford the deductibles of their policy, health care is essentially unlimited. They can check in at any institution in the United States and engage the world's greatest experts to review and treat their case. This is the most expensive form of health insurance. The HMO patient pays lower premiums and in return is entitled to care from the doctors and specialists who serve that HMO. HMOs provide discounted health care costs in return for a guaranteed income and sequestered patients. Needing a referral to a distant center for a complex or unusual disease may be a problem, depending upon the willingness of the HMO to fund such needs or even to perceive that they may exist. Getting sick away from home may also constitute a real problem, depending upon the attitude and contractual arrangement the patient has with his HMO.

Preferred Provider Organizations (PPOs) are set up to offer discounted health care in return for keeping patients in the community to receive that health care. If a patient needs very specialized care for some catastrophic event and goes to a specialist or medical center "not on the list" of chosen providers, they must often pay a deductible of 25 to 40 percent. How much would that be on a total bill of $100,000—a little more than one might prefer to spend. "Managed" health care— HMOs, PPOs, EPOs (Exclusive Provider Agents)"—offer discounted health care in return for the implicit guarantee that you will receive your care from them. The downside from a patient's point of view may be less access to highly specialized care. From the standpoint of our nation, the downside may be the loss of national medical treasures such as the Mayo Clinic or Cleveland Clinic. These great flagship institutions serve our nation by gathering experts in severe and unusual diseases. These experts could not make a living in the community because they would not have enough cases. As a people, we could not receive treatment for these problems, except through such centers. Yet, without free referral from our communities, these centers may cease to exist.

Medicare

Medical access for Medicare patients has been simple. They have almost universal access to those services covered. (A chapter later on deals entirely with Medicare.) As the budgetary process of the United States tightens, Congress must deal with two pressures vis-a-vis Medicare. First, the desire of recipients to pay the least possible out of pocket in the face of a growing national deficit. And second, the need of medical providers for certain levels of reimbursement to maintain health care delivery.

Now, Congress has enacted **prospective payment reform** or the **resource based value system**, which is a system of wage and price controls. These controls on medical services replace the free market system of determining prices. The fees have been determined by the theoretical research of a Harvard Public Health physician. Unfortunately, the health care system is complex. If such a system is fully enacted, as planed by 1996, some needed services may become inaccessible. The lessons of socialism and the history of capitalism show that in such circumstances services that are undervalued will simply disappear despite community need. When new people are retrained to provide for their needs, they will do so only at great cost due to the artificially created scarcity. Remember what happens historically in communities that practice rent control. Initially, apartments are cheap; but as time passes and no new apartments are built, prices are driven up because of the artificial scarcity.

The Indigent

Perhaps access for the truly indigent provided by Medicaid is better than access for the *almost* truly indigent but uninsured. Those with Medicaid receive those services that Medicaid provides (see the section on Medicaid) from those providers willing to accept Medicaid. The almost truly indigent who cannot pay must throw themselves on the mercy of community health care providers, while many community hospitals are already flirting with bankruptcy. This unfortunate combination insures that illness will transform the almost truly indigent into truly indigent. Their few remaining assets will be spent for their health care but their health care providers will still be brought closer to bankruptcy because the recovery made from the almost indigent does not come close to paying for the care given. This is a volatile situation that can only lead to bitterness and misunderstanding on all sides.

Reverse 'Managed' Health Care

Managed care—the HMOs, PPOs, EPOs—seeks to sequester health care delivery dollars for certain community provider groups at the possible expense of the great referral centers. Congress is presently entertaining a national system of providers as a cost saving tool. Such a system might look at big-ticket items such as a coronary bypass and designate that all Medicare patients who need such treatment go to certain specialized designated centers that would be "low bidders" for service provision. Since 70 percent of people who receive heart surgery are covered by Medicare, nondesignated centers would shut down. On the surface, this might not be all bad. In practice, one of the authors of this book works at a 500 bed hospital. He provides coronary bypasses at lower than the national mortality rates at costs less than the national average. Approximately 20 percent of all cases are done on an emergency basis. These patients would not be served at all unless they were fortunate enough to live near a designated center. Balloon dilatations, either elective or as an aggressive attempt to save some heart muscle, could not be done at nondesignated centers because they need a cardiac surgery program for back-up. This cost saving proposal of designated centers functions as a "reversed managed care" system. It has the potential to destroy community-based medical centers while creating mammoth gorillas out of our flag ship medical centers. These great centralized facilities will feed upon dollars that used to be spent in our home community. They will provide superb health care only to those who in time of extreme illness have the physical strength and financial resources to travel to them.

The Debate

This crisis has stirred a national medical debate. National debate in our society often translates into strident vocalization of special interest groups to somewhat confused nonphysician politicians. The authors favor a solution within the framework of a free market system economy. See Figure 9.1 for a comparison of Medicare and Medicaid.

Figure 9.1   Comparison

Medicare — Medicaid

To clearly distinguish between Medicare and Medicaid is to compare the salient provisions of Medicare to Medicaid:

Provision	Medicare	Medicaid
Legislation	Covered in Title 18 of the Social Security Act	Covered in Title 19 of the Social Security Act
Eligibility	People age 65 and over (regardless of need), and the disabled	Certain kinds of needy people: a) the aged b) the blind c) Aid to Families with Dependant Children
Type of Program	An insurance program	An assistance program
Funding	Pay-as-you-go	Pay-as-you-go
Sources of Funds	Social Security Taxes	Social Security Taxes, federal, state, and local taxes (federal funds normally exceed state and local funds
Governmental Agency	A federal program	A federal/state joint program
Administering Body	Federal government	State government with guidelines given by the federal government under Title 19

Chapter 10

Health Maintenance Organizations

HMOs (Health Maintenance Organizations) were developed in response to the rising cost of conventional insurance. Many people feel that fee-for-service medicine dispenses too much health care. HMOs offer a more balanced program that discourages a surfeit of tests and surgical procedures. HMO membership is certainly reasonable so long as the participant understands its philosophy, advantages, and shortcomings.

An HMO is a prepaid plan that delivers comprehensive health care for an established premium. Under the HMO system, a physician's compensation is either a fixed salary or is based upon the number of persons enrolled rather than services rendered.

Types of HMOs

The federal government has divided HMOs into three models (staff, medical group, and individual practice association), according to the relationship between an HMO and the physicians who provide services to its members.

Staff Model: Under the **staff model plan**, physicians and other health care professionals are organized as a partnership, professional corporation, or other association, working under a written contract with one or more HMOs. Although its physicians are not employees of the HMO, such a model is also a closed panel, since participants cannot receive covered medical care elsewhere. The medical group is paid a fixed per capita rate for the enrollment it serves. Income derived from these enrollment fees is then distributed to group members according to an established schedule.

Physicians may join a staff model or group model HMO for a variety of reasons. Some reasons include freedom from the business aspects of medical practice, the monetary relationship between physician and patient, the certainty of a guaranteed income, established hours and responsibilities, and a built-in consultation network.

Individual Practice Association Model: Although, like the other models, an **individual practice association model** (IPA) arranges the delivery of health care services, its physician members are not restricted to treatment of HMO participants. They may continue as private or group practitioners. Hence, this system is called an "open panel" because any physician may join an IPA.

Health care professionals provide their services according to a compensation agreement with the IPA. The participating physician agrees to a fee schedule. Included in this agreement is a provision to withhold a portion of the physician's fee to establish a reserve account in case costs of care exceeds estimates. This is called "risk sharing." Some HMOs hold physicians financially liable for the cost of medical care beyond targeted amounts. At the end of the year, if the medical utilization has been within projected guidelines, a physician may receive the balance up to 100 percent of his claims. Because physicians participating in the IPA model are located all across the country, they are unable to share records, equipment, and staff. However, peer review is still observed.

IPAs may be HMOs situated in smaller communities where the patient load of the IPA may not justify full-time employment of certain types of specialists or where community members might be unwilling to leave their long-term family physician for an HMO arrangement, but would be willing to join if their care were contracted back to their own physician. Though compensation for patient care is generally less than on a fee-for-service basis, many established physicians may enroll rather than forfeit patients with whom they have established longstanding relationships. To the new physician starting in practice, an HMO contract to care for a designated number of patients will provide the physician a guaranteed income to cover overhead. The physician may decrease their commitment to the HMO as the number of private patients increases.

On the other hand, many physicians have chosen to avoid involvement with HMOs altogether. Some fear the loss of both individual control and freedom of choice for their patients. Others are simply uncomfortable with the external control measures imposed by the quality assurance and utilization review systems of HMOs. In either case, it is the attitude and common purpose of patient and physician that ultimately determine the quality of care and that help to achieve an acceptable and reasonable result.

Problems with HMO Physicians

In a large HMO, with full-time employed physicians, health care premiums are distributed to the physician as a fixed salary, regardless of how much health care he provides. Or, as will be seen, he may even be penalized financially for referring patients to specialists.

For example, a salaried HMO physician who has been called late at night for an emergency room consultation may elect not to see the patient but instead to provide a telephone consultation. Their salary, however, will remain unchanged. On the other hand, a private fee-for-service physician who does not report to the emergency room in such a situation will not be reimbursed. Of course, both specialists, if they are physicians of integrity, will respond appropriately but the HMO physician will not suffer an economic loss if the response is not in person.

The HMO physician with fixed salary maximizes the compensation as they do the least work and deliver the least amount of health care. Under traditional arrangements, physicians paid for services rendered must maximize their standard of living by being more productive—by delivering more health care.

In a smaller HMO, the family practitioner may provide care for a certain number of HMO patients as well as their own fee-for-service patients. In such a system, they will receive a capitation rate for each HMO member, whether treated or not. The more HMO patients they see, the less time they will have available for private patients who pay for each appointment. By dispensing the least possible time and care to their HMO patients, the physician will have the maximum amount of time to spend with private or fee-for-service patients, which will increase their income.

The HMO patient must be aware of these economic incentives and be prepared to demand needed health care just as the fee-for-service patient must avoid being sold too much health care by unscrupulous physicians.

Problems with the HMO System

The essence of the HMO system is a fixed, prepaid premium in return for comprehensive health care services. HMOs charge less than fee-for-service plans; otherwise, they would have no competitive attraction. They also have heavier administrative and advertising budgets than the traditional fee-for-service system.

Because HMOs function in a free enterprise society, they face the threat of insolvency and disintegration unless they make a profit. In order to deliver health care at a lower cost and still remain profitable, HMOs have three choices:

1. Reducing payment to physicians may be a solution providing the quality of service is maintained.
2. Rationing service is also an alternative. The participants in less expensive programs must recognize that, in return for lower premiums, they are enrolled in a health care system whose incentives favor dispensing less care.
3. Insuring only good risk patients in order to reach their economic goals.

Of the three methods listed, only the last solution is fundamentally unjust. It removes low risk patients from traditional insurance risk pools while rejecting higher risk patients. Such cost control raises premiums for individuals enrolled in traditional insurance programs. These people are burdened with the health care costs of the high risk patients remaining after HMOs have enrolled the young low risk candidates. Such an adverse selection could drive the cost of other health care programs beyond the reach of the American people or indeed of the United States government.

Advantages of the HMO System

Reduced costs are the primary advantage of HMOs. Young individuals in a low risk group, for example, will find their premiums relatively inexpensive because their need for highly specialized health care is less likely.

A well-run HMO reduces the probability of redundant tests and unnecessary surgery. The whole structure of the system discourages it. Furthermore, HMOs support their regional economies by gathering their patient population for care in local participating hospitals. This is especially important in a time when many small hospitals are threatened with bankruptcy.

Weaknesses of the HMO System

Because members must select their physicians from among those participating in HMO programs, they may need to give up their family physicians or specialists whose names are not on the HMO list. In addition, a patient with an unusual disease will be more likely to be treated nearer his home than transferred to the care of a medical expert who practices some distance away. HMOs sequester members for the benefit of the local economy, which forces insured Americans to give up the wide range of freedom which previously allowed them to select physician, specialist, and site of treatment.

Becoming ill away from home can be a problem. A patient who suffered a cardiac arrest while driving through town was resuscitated and brought to the Coronary Care Unit. Two days later, it was discovered that he belonged to an HMO in a city 150 miles away. When contacted, his HMO denied the admitting hospital any reimbursement for care already provided because there had been no preadmission clearance. Furthermore, although the attending cardiologist wanted to assess the risks of another cardiac arrest and the need for coronary bypass, the HMO recommended that the patient be returned to his local hospital for such testing procedures despite his unstable condition. The admitted cardiologist was left to face the dilemma of keeping and testing the patient at a loss of thousands of dollars to himself and the hospital or allowing an unstable patient to seek some means of transport to get him 150 miles to the area covered by his HMO. Transportation costs, incidently, were neither provided or supported by his HMO. What would you have done?

Moral, social, and economic rewards in a society should encourage excellence and achievement. Some staff model HMOs provide fixed, secure salaries that offer no incentive for productivity or excellence among physicians. Some gatekeeper HMOs impose penalties in the form of salary or bonus reductions for tests, diagnostic procedures, or specialized care that a member physician might recommend. Under some HMO programs, the physician who dispenses too much health care could generate a negative take-home salary (i.e., owe the HMO).

As a participant in one capitated gatekeeper model HMO, a physician receives $4 per month for each patient and he can ask for 1,000, 2,000, 3,000 or 4,000 patients. He is given a fund to cover laboratory tests, consultations to specialists, surgery, and hospitalization. In this case, the funds are set to support 250 hospital days per 1,000 patients per year. In the United States, the general population averages about 500 hospital days per 1,000 patients per year, while in the Medicare population the average is 1,000 hospital days per 1,000 patients per year. If he sees no one, the physician receives a bonus from all unused funds at the end of the year. However, as he exceeds consultations and hospitalizations of 250 days per 1,000 patients per year, the excess cost per patient is deducted from his salary. The physician is ultimately responsible for his hospital fund. If he exceeds his target by too much, he might owe the HMO.

Since the HMO allocates only one-half the average number of hospital days prescribed nationally under this system, the average physician would be short of funds in June. Consider a hypothetical HMO patient who complains of chest pain, which the doctor feels might result from an impending heart attack. Knowing that he has used the average number of hospital days for his patients and has already depleted his various funds, the doctor has two choices. He could send this patient to a cardiologist. However, since his HMO testing fund has been depleted, his salary will be reduced if the cardiologist performs a stress test and a cardiac catheterization. Such studies might reveal blockage in the arteries to the patient's heart so severe that sudden death could result. These blockages might require balloon dilatation or a coronary bypass for their correction. The patient may well regain a normal life expectancy but will have a somewhat impoverished doctor whose reduced salary reflects both the cardiologist and surgeon fees and hospital costs. Instead of referring this patient for specialized cardiac evaluation and care, the physician could prescribe an inexpensive nitroglycerin tablet. If the pain disappeared, the patient could be continued on medical care rather than sending them for further costly testing and treatment. If a sudden fatal heart attack occurred, the physician would lose only $4 per month. Of course, no responsible physician would ever compromise his patient in such a manner. This example is meant only to illustrate one of the pitfalls of the system.

In fact, most capitated HMO physicians try to manage what problems they can without specialized referral. Then to protect their somewhat limited funds, they select tests carefully, admit patients on the day of surgery (rather than the night before), and encourage their specialists to press for "early as safe" hospital dismissal to preserve those precious hospital days and their own reduced livelihood.

Sometimes HMO patients become severely ill. A young man from a small town recently underwent emergency heart surgery and prolonged hospitalization. In order to minimize liability to the HMO, the local physicians had pooled their hospital funds but this patient was so ill that the costs of his care depleted their remaining HMO hospital allowances. The young man survived and eventually returned to work, but his HMO physicians were severely penalized for offering good care and their salaries were put on the line for all their other HMO patients that year. If your support funds were exhausted early in the year and your take home salary was liable for all further referrals for specialized care, how would you handle the next and all subsequent patients who need specialized referral? (Remember that the HMO may often constitute more than 40 percent of a physician's patient base.)

To summarize, HMOs came into existence to help cope with the high cost of health care. Utilization of services is the single most important factor in determining the size of the health care bill. HMOs were established to deliver health care in an environment that encourages the physician to dispense less, rather than more, thus controlling cost. Despite its disadvantages, unless the more traditional forms of coverage are radically reformed to control cost, the HMO and managed health care are the wave of the future.

Chapter 11

Medicare and Long-Term Care

In 1965, Medicare was made part of the Social Security System, a mandatory federal retirement and benefit program to which all Americans contribute throughout their working years. Social Security funds are accumulated not through an irrevocable trust or a contract with an insurance company, but from automatic salary deductions that are matched by employers and continue until a changing higher level of income is reached. Medicare accounts for 19 percent of every Social Security tax dollar collected, and without it health care for the elderly and disabled would be rationed on the basis of ability to pay.

Medicare Beneficiaries

The elderly and disabled are direct beneficiaries of Medicare. There are many indirect beneficiaries. Medicare payments of health care costs have relieved many sons and daughters of the financial obligation of their elderly parents. No doubt this relief has helped raise the standard of living for this middle-aged group and has helped many of their children realize a college education or has enhanced their personal standard of living.

Since the passage of Medicare in 1965, the system has provided our hospitals with a continuing flow of funds. Without Medicare funds, many hospitals would not have survived, while many others could not have expanded and improved. Certainly, there has been waste. The improved quality in medicine has been expensive, but all Americans are benefiting from these improved hospital services. Without the massive infusion of government funds through Medicare, many advanced life-saving services and technologies would not be available. Medicare has helped to free physicians from having to choose therapy consistent with the patient's ability to pay. Today, as a direct result of Medicare, physicians find themselves not having to ration services on the basis of the patient's income.

Medical Overview

Medicare was signed into law by President Lyndon Johnson. It was part of his concept for the program of the "Great Society." Developing a strategy to evaluate short-, intermediate-, and long-term health care should be part of every citizen's thinking. As one approaches Medicare eligibility, it is important to understand what Medicare does and does not provide. Anyone who does not understand Medicare benefits leaves himself/herself at risk of being underinsured. They will also be vulnerable to over buying of commercial Medicare supplements without receiving additional coverage or providing for the cost of nursing home care.

Eligibility for Medicare

You are eligible for Medicare if:

1. You are 65 or older (even if you are still working and are not insured under Social Security.
2. You are disabled and entitled to Social Security benefits for at least 24 months.
3. You or your dependents suffer from chronic kidney failure for which you require dialysis or transplant.
4. You are receiving unskilled medical care such as a nursing home or custodial care.

Medicare has two parts: Hospital (Part A) and Medical Insurance (Part B).

Let's look at Part A, which pays for hospitalization. The government used to pay 80 percent of a hospital's charges for treatment of a sick patient. Now the government has switched to the **DRG system**, which allows a fixed payment for each patient based on the admitting diagnosis. The payment is based on national averages and bears no relationship to the cost of treating an individual case. A hospital's survival depends upon its ability to treat each type of case at less than the national average cost. Avoidance of bankruptcy may depend upon earlier patient dismissals.

Under the new philosophy, the sick individual will remain in the hospital only so long as simpler less expensive care is inadequate. The patient is no longer kept in the hospital until they feel good, but only until dismissal is safe. Briefer hospital stays can result in one of several dispositions.

Home Health Care

Medicare Part A pays for home health care *only* when skilled treatment by trained personnel is required. This might include part-time nursing care, physical therapy, medical social services, use of medical supplies (not drugs or other medications), and some rehabilitation equipment for use on an outpatient basis. Generally, a patient need not be hospitalized before becoming eligible for home health service benefits. Coinsurance applies in home health care.

Medicare Part A does not pay for services that people without professional training could provide. Furthermore, individual cases are routinely reviewed by a utilization review committee composed of doctors, nurses, and other medical professionals whose recommendations may determine the continuation of these services.

Skilled Nursing Care

A skilled nursing facility is a nursing home that provides skilled care or rehabilitation services under the direction of a doctor. Before a patient can enter such an institution, his or her transfer must be ordered by the doctor and approved by the medical review board. Medicare will not pay for treatment that does not require such professional supervision.

Skilled care must be provided by a licensed individual, such as a nurse or physical therapist, upon a doctor's orders. Medicare Part A will help pay for skilled services, as well as for a semiprivate room, for rehabilitation services, for medical social services, for use of appliances and equipment (such as braces and wheelchairs), for drugs supplied by the skilled nursing facility, for nursing services, and for all meals and special diets.

Custodial Care

Do not confuse skilled care with custodial care that helps meet a patient's personal needs such as taking a bath, eating, walking, taking medicine, or getting into and out of bed. These services are not provided by Medicare. Unless you plan to pay for these out of pocket, other insurance coverage must be found.

Hospice Care

Although a hospice does not offer curative treatment, it does provide pain relief, symptom management, support devices, and counseling to terminally ill patients and their families. These services, typically coordinated for both inpatient, outpatient, and home care, qualify for coinsurance and Medicare. Reimbursable allowances for the terminally ill patient include physician services, nursing care, medical social services, homemaker/home health aid services, short-term inpatient care, and outpatient drugs for pain relief.

Respite Care

This is a short-term inpatient stay offering temporary relief to the person who regularly provides home care. There is, however, a maximum number of consecutive days for each respite.

Not all hospitals participate in Medicare Part A. Some of the major exclusions shared by Part A and Part B include:

- Cosmetic surgery
- Personal comfort items
- Items covered by Worker's compensation
- Routine checkups
- Eye examinations and glasses
- Hearing aids
- Services outside the United States

- Custodial care
- Acupuncture
- War claims

There are many more exclusions. Call your local Social Security Office for a detailed listing.

Medicare Part B—Medical Insurance

Having Medicare Part A (hospital and skilled care coverage) makes you eligible for Medicare Part B, which helps pay physician and surgeon bills as well as regular office visits. Unlike Part A, which is paid for by the Medicare part of the general social security fund, you must pay a premium for part of the cost of Part B coverage. This payment or premium is deducted from social security checks, railroad retirement benefits, and civil service annuities. Otherwise, to be eligible, quarterly payment subject to annual increases must be made directly to the Health Care Finance Administration. Everyone eligible should subscribe to Medicare "Part B." First, it helps pay for essential parts of health care. And second, 75 percent of the actual cost of these services is subsidized by the general health care fund. Your premium represents only 25 percent of the actual cost of care provided to beneficiaries.

The Payment System

The payment system under Medicare Part B is complex enough to confuse even gifted individuals. The bottom line is you should receive care from providers who accept Medicare assignment whenever possible. The individual who patronizes providers who do not accept Medicare will transfer to those providers a much more significant portion of their personal wealth.

Watching the Money Go

Medicare says it will provide coinsurance (i.e., pay) 80 percent of the *approved amount* of the health care provider's charges. The recipient of the health care services must pay the balance. Now, the usual bright-eyed recipient quickly calculates that this leaves them 20 percent of the bill. This conclusion is reached because it was learned in school that 80 percent plus 20 percent equal 100 percent, and 100 percent is perceived as being the whole bill. Well, if one's provider "accepts assignment" that may be true, but if the chosen provider does not accept assignment, even magic could not make your money disappear faster.

Approved amount is the key. Suppose the fair market value of health care services rendered (i.e., the amount that would be billed to the individual covered by private insurance) is $1,000. No one says Medicare has to approve $1,000 for those services. In fact and in practice, Medicare may approve the amount of only $500. Now the health care provider (the physician/the surgeon) may wince a bit when they see what they believe to be $1,000 worth of services devalued by their political cousins to $500. However, if they accept Medicare assignment, they must accept $500 as full payment. Medicare will pay 80 percent or $400, and you the recipient will pay 20 percent or $100—net cost to you $100.

If the nonmathematically inclined ill person receives those same healing ministrations from a provider who does not accept assignment, they will receive the same bill for $1,000 from the provider. They submit the bill to Medicare but discover the "approved amount" is only $500, of which Medicare will pay 80 percent or $400. Since the provider in this case does not accept assignment, this leaves a sick patient with a balance of $600, which may make them wince but the provider smile. That's how the money disappears. To avoid financial woes that may dampen your recovery, choose providers who *accept* assignment.

If the physician accepts Medicare assignment, the government will pay him directly and the patient will be billed for 20 percent of the allowed amount. If the physician does not accept assignment, Medicare will send the patient the check for 80 percent of the "approved amount." The patient who received the services then has the obligation to pay the physician charges that may come to several times the approved amount.

Major Services Covered by Medicare Part B:

- Medical and surgical services, including anesthesia
- Diagnosis and treatment in a doctor's office
- Diagnostic tests and procedures connected with treatment
- Outpatient x-rays if ordered by a physician
- Medical equipment prescribed by a physician
- Approved "minor" surgery that can be performed in certified walk-in surgical centers

- Drugs that cannot be self-administered
- Prosthetic devices
- Second opinions when surgery is recommended

Some Services NOT Covered by Medicare Part B:

- Routine physical examinations
- Hearing examinations or hearing aids
- Eye examinations or eyeglasses
- Dental care unless related to surgery of the jaw
- Routine foot care
- Cosmetic surgery

Medicare GAP

Obviously, Medicare has its problems. The concept of assignment, the scope of covered services, and the nature of reimbursement can be irritating and confusing. Part B itself contains some serious shortcomings: the deductible amount, the 20 percent coinsurance, the sum beyond Medicare's approved amount on nonassigned claims, and noncovered services.

These areas are called the **Medicare GAP** and even participants with adequate financial resources should consider covering such gaps with supplemental insurance. Just be sure that the supplement you pay for fills the gaps that you need. It is senseless to pay for services already provided under Medicare.

If you are confused, seek help from you employer, the State Department of Insurance, or state and area agencies on aging. Many states offer assistance in filling out claim forms and in evaluating Medicare GAP insurance as well as individual health needs.

Medicare—an Operational Look

When a patient enters a participating hospital, they are assigned a disposition category called a **Diagnostic Related Group** (DRG) that determines Medicare's reimbursement to that hospital. Because compensation is based upon diagnosis rather than the cost of care, a hospital will receive the same amount for two patients admitted with identical diagnoses, although the expenses involved for each might be quite different.

Consider, for example, a 65-year-old male who goes to the hospital emergency room with chest pain. He is recently retired and is now on Medicare. He maintains an active lifestyle. He is involved in many community activities. Testing is performed and he is found to have coronary artery disease that will require surgery. Coronary bypass is performed. He is released from the hospital in a relatively short period of time. The hospital makes money on this case.

Now, consider an 83-year-old male, a retired university professor in the process of writing his third book. He is also quite active. He goes to the emergency room with chest pain and is also found to have life-threatening coronary disease that requires surgery. Studies show that elective coronary bypass surgery in patients over the age of 80 is associated with no major increase in mortality, but hospitalizations may be longer. This is the case with the professor who does well but does not recover as rapidly as the younger man. The hospital will, therefore, lose money on this case. Does the DRG system then discourage delivering health care to the very elderly?

The goals of the DRG system are admirable. A first class, efficient hospital would prosper. An inefficient or poor hospital would either refer their sicker patients to the more efficient institution or go bankrupt. Patients will be given the best care at the best hospitals while the poorer, less efficient institutions may fall by the wayside. Quality triumphs.

Now, let's see how the system really works. As hospitals throughout the nation burdened with tight profit margins struggle to survive, they face the difficult decision of whether to discontinue services reimbursed by the less profitable DRGs, no matter how needed or necessary these may be in the community. The hospital may be forced to ration or eliminate a needed but under-funded service in order to survive. Should the hospital ration or eliminate nonprofitable services to concentrate its advertising and resources on better reimbursed services, thus insuring its survival? In high paying DRGs, such as cardiac (heart related), will the hospital be tempted to ration services based on age (denying complex procedures to the older DRG group to enhance profit margins) or will the hospital deny services to the younger but very sick DRG patient whose needed services will far exceed what the Medicare DRG will pay?

The concept of spending an equal amount of money on all patients with the same problem won't work. A young healthy person who needs surgery for a specific problem may recover quickly. An elderly, frail person may take much longer to recover from the insult of surgery.

During that time, the frail person will consume more resources and more health care dollars.

A major fallacy of the present DRG system is that the government bases its "lump sum" payment on what it feels should be the average cost of caring for Medicare patients across the spectrum of age and frailty. If the amounts allotted were sufficient to cover costs, there would be no problems. Unfortunately, most hospitals in the United States lose money on Medicare patients. What alternatives do these hospitals have to survive? They can discontinue the needed service. They can "cost shift" charging private patients more. And, they can deny performance of the service to the frail and elderly who are likely to be nonprofitable members of each DRG class.

Historically, we have seen a few hospitals discontinue services. Most hospitals practice cost shifting to cover expenses. But as individuals and corporations can no longer afford their rising health care bills, they now negotiate strict cost control into their health care plans. Either the government will be forced to pay for the health care it has promised or, if hospitals are to survive, they will resort to internal health care rationing based on age and physical condition.

It does not appear that the federal government plans to increase DRG spending. The **Health Care Financing Agency** (HCFA), the funding arm of Medicare, is already taking steps to ration health care to the very ill. First, through the **resource-based relative value system** (RBRVS), the government will decrease payments to highly trained specialists who perform complex procedures. As reimbursement decreases, availability will decrease. The stated intention of the RBRVS is to raise compensation to family practitioners who provide desperately needed but less expensive basic care. Tax what you would eliminate. Subsidize what you would have grow.

Second, the government discourages delivery of health care to the aged and the frail by publishing mortality and morbidity statistics of hospitals and physicians by DRG group but without regard to the condition of the individual patient in each group. For example, if a hospital's death rate for performing coronary bypass is to be published in the newspaper, will a surgeon offer bypass surgery to the 81-year-old who needs it but might ruin the statistics? Coronary bypass done on an otherwise healthy individual with coronary artery disease should carry a risk of less than one percent. The same operation done on a patient having a massive heart attack and in shock may carry a risk of over 50 percent. How does the provider explain this to the local newspaper? Or, does he or she eliminate the service to this very sick class of individuals?

If we eliminate surgery for the very sick patient, the cost of health care will go down. If we eliminate surgery for the high risk patient, our mortality statistics will improve. Lay people read in the newspaper of better mortality rates achieved by a particular hospital and they want to go there. Albeit, the better statistics are achieved by denying surgery to very sick patients. Lay people never consider themselves as very sick anyway.

By failing to differentiate the severity of illness of patients undergoing various procedures and then publishing results, a hospital or practitioner may look better if they consciously or unconsciously ration care to those most likely to have a good result—irrespective of their need. This may be what our society wants. It may be all we can afford, but we should face the issues honestly and make this decision openly. We should not come to this philosophy of health care by destroying hospitals and physicians who persist in caring for very frail, elderly, and critically ill patients.

The DRG Ideal and Bracket Creep

The ideal of the DRG system is to publish a fixed rate of reimbursement so that hospitals can quickly determine the profitability of certain cases. If a hospital cannot make a profit within a given DRG, it must decide whether to suffer a financial loss or transfer such cases to another more efficient institution. In theory, these economic pressures would lead all patients to be treated in the best, most efficient hospital environment. Realistically, less profitable services are simply being dropped regardless of medical need. In fact, a whole new layer of bureaucracy has been created. Computer programs and DRG analysts sift through the patient's many diagnoses to determine which will pay the most money. Often the same procedure can be interpreted differently, which yields payment differences of thousands of dollars. The admitting physician is asked to review the chart after the patient's dismissal. Under oath, jeopardy of perjury, and criminal prosecution, he or she is asked to sign a statement indicating that this most expensive DRG interpretation was the principal reason for this particular hospitalization. The physician has the right to refuse to sign the face sheet or to change it. He or she knows that almost all hospitals in the United States lost money last year on the DRGs. He or she knows that if they compound their hospital's loss that it may go bankrupt.

Caring for too many severely ill patients threatens a hospital with insolvency. The temptation, therefore, is to select only good risk patients in each category, which will promote earlier dismissals and increase profit. It is theoretically possible to gain the greatest profit simply by selecting patients with recoverable diagnoses and then dismissing them with essentially no treatment. The ultimate inducement of the DRG system, however, is to sell health care to the youngest, healthiest Medicare patients who can be labeled with high paying DRG titles and at the same time withhold care from the feeble and seriously ill— all to avoid financial loss.

A system that discourages extending care to the very ill is unacceptable. A system that rewards hospitals for admitting the best risk patients and giving them the least possible care is irrational. A system that bankrupts institutions that provide the best care to the very ill is wrong.

It is fortunate that most hospitals and physicians maintain their integrity. They continue to deliver good health care to the seriously ill but only at a financial loss, or more exactly, by shifting costs to the private payer.

Long-Term Care/Nursing Home Care

Long-Term Care (LTC) is a service that covers a broad spectrum of definitions. In general, LTC is defined as medical and support services provided on a sustained basis to us, when we cannot function independently because of a chronic illness or condition. Those people at greatest risk to LTC are the very aged, often chronically, mentally ill singles. Women far outnumber men in nursing homes, accounting for almost two-thirds of the nursing home population. This information should suprise no one, given the fact that women tend to have a longer life span than men.

Unlike other areas of life-cycle planning, such as retirement planning, health care planning, disability income, and group term life insurance, LTC planning has not been included in the core corporate employee benefits package. Today, there is a major marketing thrust, spearheaded by the insurance industry, to include LTC plans into the corporate world of employee benefits. This effort is clearly being supported by our federal government, which is now publishing General Accounting Office (GAO) reports dealing with LTC insurance models. We do not believe that LTC deserves to be given this level of recognition.

If the federal government is disturbed by the "enormous liabilities" encompassing LTC, then a simple solution would be to change federal and state tax laws to allow us to establish individual LTC retirement accounts similar to the Individual Retirement Account (IRA), under *Section 408* of the Internal Revenue Code. Contributions could be made using before tax dollars, and interest accumulations would be either tax-deferred or tax-exempt. Those of us who do not require LTC would ultimately pay taxes on the balance of funds in our LTC account. Those of us requiring LTC would use the accumulated funds, without paying taxes on either the amount contributed to our LTC account, or on the interest earnings from these contributed funds.

Background

Long-Term Care insurance policies typically offer indemnity benefits for nursing care. These policies pay a set amount each day for a specific period of time that we receive care. A policy may or may not cover all types of LTC (generally termed as skilled, intermediate, and custodial care), and policies may define covered LTC services or facilities differently. Many policies also cover home health care services, which can refer to skilled nursing care provided at home by medical professionals. Home health care services can also refer to assistance with such daily living activities as eating and bathing, which can be provided by people without medical skills.

Traditionally, states have had the primary responsibility for regulating the insurance industry. State insurance agencies are linked through the National Association of Insurance Commissioners (NAIC), which is composed of the heads of the state agencies. In 1986, NAIC established model standards that have evolved rapidly since that time. Although the standards are not mandatory, they suggest the minimum standards states should adopt for regulating LTC insurance. Today, the standards also provide increased consumer protection, while offering insurance companies flexibility to experiment with different products in a competitive, emerging market.

Because states have the responsibility for setting LTC insurance standards, they must determine the balance between our protection as consumers and the insurance industry's need for flexibility. An appropriate balance is difficult to achieve. For example, limitations in LTC insurance policies can reduce both benefit eligibility and the benefits available. To the extent that such limitations are removed and coverage increased, however, policy prices can increase to levels that are unaffordable for many of us.

The LTC insurance industry is a new development within the past 15 years, so insurance companies generally have inadequate experience data to establish stable policy prices. Premiums can vary as much as 150 percent for policies with similar benefits. Thus, we face great financial risks when selecting the proper LTC insurance plan for our needs. Periodic price adjustments could also make it difficult for us to retain our policies, and those of us who allow our policies to lapse almost always lose the investment component of our premiums.

On average, insurance companies expect 60 percent or more of their original policyholders to allow their LTC policies to lapse within ten years. In all but a very few exceptions, we, the policyholders, lose out in a big way, unless the insurance company provides nonforfeiture benefits. Nonforfeiture benefits provide a return of a portion of the reserves resulting from our premium payments, should we allow our LTC policies to lapse. For example, if we purchase a policy without nonforfeiture benefits at age 75, we would on average lose all, or nearly $20,000 in premiums paid if we allowed the policy to lapse at age 85. This $20,000 loss represents premiums only and ignores the time value loss of our money (earnings). On the other hand, we would receive back about $12,000 to $14,000 of the $20,000 paid in premiums with a nonforfeiture benefit included in the policy. Unfortunately, NAIC standards do not require insurance companies to offer nonforfeiture benefits, so the existence of these benefits in LTC insurance policies is still the exception. Nevertheless, given a nonforfeiture clause in our LTC policy, substantial losses would still be incurred; as in our example, we would lose $6,000 to $8,000 of our money in premiums paid alone, not to mention our time value of money losses.

Premiums/Pricing LTC Policies

Insurance companies base policy premiums on several major actuarial assumptions. Some of these assumptions are:

1. The expenses the insurance company expects to incur, such as sales commissions, state premium taxes (all insurance products sold in the United States have state premium taxes)
2. Anticipated claims
3. Anticipated lapse rate

4. Earnings—this is the anticipated interest rate the insurance company expects to receive on reserves. The higher the earning assumption used by the insurance company, the lower the premium the insurance company will charge for LTC coverage. The lower the earning assumption used by the insurance company, the higher the premium the company will charge for LTC coverage. Therefore, it should surprise no one that insurance companies historically use low earning assumptions when pricing nearly all of its products.
5. Insurance company profits
6. Risk charges
7. Administrative charges.

Another important factor is our age at the time that we purchase a LTC policy from an insurance company. The annual premium for a 70-year-old consumer would be much greater than the premium paid by a 35-year-old consumer. This example is a simple reflection on time value of money.

Those of us who obtain LTC insurance at the lowest market price cannot be sure that the policy will remain a bargain. Under NAIC standards, insurers can increase premiums on existing policies. Thus, insurance companies can transfer from themselves to us a substantial portion of the risk associated with LTC insurance; that is, insurers who incur more claims than expected can simply increase premiums.

Premium increases can place us at risk of being priced out of the market at the time when we are at greatest risk for needing LTC services. The risk of future premium increases may be significant, given that some insurers may initially underprice policies because of the extremely competitive market. Low initial prices work to our advantage only if insurers do not raise prices significantly in the future. However, pricing policies in a new market without data on the use of LTC services will require insurers to make adjustments.

Convert Our Home

One of the authors has a neighbor who has successfully created his own nursing home "within" his home. The individual is elderly, single, and chronically ill. He has altered his home to accomodate his needs and to utilize the many home-health and elder care services that are available. Such alterations require planning and spending of some dollars.

Cost comparison of home care with nursing homes or continuing care retirement communities may prove that home owners may be better off to consider what our neighbor has discovered: stay home. The fact that he remains in his home and within the confines of his environment would seem to be a real emotional plus.

More information for establishing your own nursing home, at home, can be obtained by contacting your State Aging and Adult Services Department. Look in your telephone book.

We believe that increased medical technologies, including, but not limited to, by-pass surgery, drug therapy, eye surgery, artificial joints and organ transplants, will all contribute in enabling elderly people who would formerly have been nursing home candidates to avoid such institutionalization. Increasing home health and elder care services and case management refinement will undoubtedly shrink the percentage of our population requiring nursing home care. This shrinkage in demand will be dramatic, possibly including only the chronically, mentally ill as ultimately requiring long-term care. It seems difficult to imagine anyone comfortably investing hard-earned money in an insurance policy that guarantees some LTC benefits in the future. The LTC market presents a strong potential for decreasing demand for nursing home facilities, which will result in a reduction of risk to the individual consumer. It would seem reasonable that a majority of us, not yet retired and those retired, would be far better off financially to save our dollars prudently in a personal investment account rather than make premium payments for years. It is difficult to conclude that premium payments are justified by the benefit return, if any.

If we are a high risk person for long-term care in a nursing home, we are precisely those people that insurance companies seek to screen out during the application and underwriting process. In other words, if we are in a high-risk category that would justify investing premiums in a long-term care policy, we may not be able to obtain one.

Chapter 12

Fee-For-Service Systems

This is clearly the best plan in times of major illness because needed specialized care is available on a need-and-use basis. Patients pay a fixed annual premium to the insurer in return for payment as used for all or part of that person's expenses. The premiums are determined by:

- The size of the pool at risk
- The age and health (i.e., risk status) of the pool members
- The cost of medical care in the geographic area
- The rate of utilization of medical care in the geographic area.

It is important to understand the mechanism of payment under this system. Individual or corporate premiums are paid to the insurer. The insurer may then invest these monies until health care is rendered. At the time that health care is rendered, the insurer is billed and the physician or hospital is reimbursed for care given. If no care is given, no payment is made. Fee-for-service has traditionally been the most common form of insurance. Fee-for-service is the gold standard by which all alternative systems should be measured.

Like each of the preceding systems, the fee-for-service system has its weaknesses:

1. Some plans provide inadequate coverage in time of need.
2. Some plans make you pay for routine doctor visits, child care, and so forth.
3. Some plans require second opinions before providing coverage for elective procedures.
4. Built-in incentives are to sell too much health care, to do too much to patients.
5. It is too costly.

Inadequate Coverage in Time of Need

Read the "fine print." Before purchasing a policy, understand exactly what it covers. Does it pay for your surgery or does it give you a set amount of money each time you have surgery performed? Will the set amount of money be enough to pay for your operations?

You Must Pay for Routine Doctor Visits

This will make you feel "nickeled and dimed" to death, but people will think twice before using a service that costs them money. It discourages over-utilization. It helps control costs.

Second Opinions Do Not Come in Second — They Are Worthless

Second opinions do not protect you from purchasing too much health care. Second opinions do not protect you from too many procedures. Consider how second opinions are given:

*   They are not impartial. They are usually given by doctors who know each other.
*   In giving a second opinion, one must consider the legitimacy of various more or less aggressive treatment philosophies.
*   The doctor giving the second opinion has as much chance of being wrong as the doctor giving the first opinion.

- Unless the recommending physician is totally incompetent, there is always support in some medical publication for any outlandish treatment. You can always find a "greater fool than thou" to support your position.
- In many systems, if one physician turns down a treatment request, it is possible for the recommending physician to steer his patients away from that physician in the future.

Here is an example of a true case concerning a corporate benefit manager whose policy required a second opinion.

The patient was a severe diabetic. He had extremely bad coronary artery disease. His heart specialist had tried for four months to maintain the patient on a stringent regimen of medicine, diet, and limitation of activity without success. The patient was deteriorating and the cardiologist felt the patient would die without surgery. He was referred to a surgeon who reviewed the data and felt that the patient was high risk but agreed with the cardiologist's conclusions. The surgeon recommended bypass surgery. The patient was then referred for a second surgical opinion. The surgeon reviewing for the second opinion recommended against performing the bypass procedure. It would be, in his mind, a very high risk procedure. The patient was then left with some doubt and confusion. One surgeon and one cardiologist told him that he would die *without* surgery. The second opinion surgeon told him that he would probably die *from* the surgery.

The insurance company requested a third opinion. The patient was then referred to a university 150 miles away. While waiting for this opinion, the patient went into congestive heart failure. He had to be readmitted to the hospital. Once the patient's heart failure was corrected, he went to the university where they agreed with the first surgeon. They felt that the surgery was indeed high risk, but that there was little alternative. Without the surgery the patient's life expectancy was very short. At this point, the insurance company would not give approval. They now had two opinions for and one opinion against surgery. The patient was then referred to a famous clinic almost 400 miles away. Before he could be seen there, he suffered several episodes of severe chest pain that were treated medically. He was again hospitalized but did not have a heart attack. The patient then made the trip to the famous clinic, which reviewed the data and agreed that surgery would be somewhat high risk, but that the patient needed the surgery at the famous clinic rather than the institution nearer his home. This introduced more doubt into the patient's mind.

While awaiting the insurance company's review of this opinion, the patient went into the hospital and was treated for another episode of congestive failure. The patient was at risk of sudden death for almost two months. Finally, approval was given and the patient underwent an uncomplicated coronary bypass at his home hospital. He returned to work after a short period of recuperation. The cost of the second opinions in this case was relatively high, not just in money but in risk to the patient who had a life-threatening illness untreated for two months.

This case highlights some of the dilemmas of the second opinion:

- Suppose the patient had died while awaiting surgery. This could create a liability situation for all parties concerned.
- A second opinion doctor recommends against surgery. The patient drops dead at work. Will the second opinion doctor be sued?
- A surgeon operates in the face of a negative second opinion. The patient has a bad result. Will the surgeon be sued?
- Even the most honest giver of second opinions will be influenced by his own experience. What is high risk to one surgery practice may not be high risk to another.

Assessment of risk will vary tremendously according to the support systems and sophistication of specialty development in an area or hospital. A procedure that could be performed safely in one hospital might be better left undone in another hospital. How would you manage treating rupture of the ascending thoracic aorta in a hospital without a heart-lung machine?

When the aorta (the main blood vessel arising from the heart) starts to rupture, the usual treatment is to go on the heart-lung machine and replace the ruptured section of the aorta. If a hospital has no heart-lung machine and the patient cannot be transferred, a daring attempt can be made to repair and wrap the aorta. The patient will almost certainly not survive. Risk changes with environment. The assessment of risks is crucial to getting an honest second opinion.

Here's another example of money being wasted on a second opinion. In some areas, if a general surgeon recommends performing a dilatation and curettage (a simple gynecological procedure) on a Medicaid patient, Medicaid demands a second opinion to make sure the procedure is indicated. Medicaid will pay the doctor giving the second opinion more than it will reimburse the surgeon for doing the procedure.

Second opinions are generally ineffective in cost control; rather, they tend to drive up costs. They are also generally ineffective in preventing so-called "unnecessary surgeries."

The Incentive to Sell Too Much, to Do Too Much

A major criticism of the fee-for-service system is the incentive to sell too much medicine—to do too much to patients. Just as the HMO system struggles with rationing, providing too little care, the private fee-for-service system struggles with the tendency to sell too much, to perform too many procedures. In fee-for-service systems, doctors only get paid if they render services. We have all heard the insinuations about doctors who perform countless tests on machines that they own in order to maximize their income. We have all heard rumors of surgeons who perform unnecessary operations. This must be controlled.

This brings up two important questions with respect to conflict of interest for physicians. The first question is the ownership of equipment. The second question is the same physician recommending the procedure, performing the procedure, and judging the quality of the procedure.

Physician Ownership of Equipment

Let's start with absolute clarity. We are not addressing the family physician who has a blood count machine or electrolyte machine in their office for convenience. We are talking about the physician who may own equipment worth millions of dollars. This equipment must be paid for. The inherent conflicts of interest are obvious. The result is that the cost of health care increases.

A physician should be allowed to own small testing equipment that will increase the convenience of medical practice by making simple data (e.g., blood counts, simple chemistries, or stress tests readily available). Many physicians perform these tests at lower costs than commercial laboratories. Furthermore, as a citizen of this country, a physician has the right to own any amount of medical equipment if this is to be his means of support, provided he does not also control referral of patients for testing on his own equipment.

Physicians should not be allowed to own "big-ticket" items such as CT scanners, million-dollar nuclear resonance scanners, and cardiac catheterization laboratories, especially if they are in a position to refer patients for testing on their own equipment. The temptation to order too many tests to make the very expensive equipment profitable would be too great for many human beings. In the case of the big-ticket items, the hospitals or third-party laboratories should own the testing equipment. The reason for ordering a test is a patient's need to have the test done. The physician should not receive a financial reward or compensation for referring patients to have tests done on this equipment. This would decrease the temptation to order tests, and equipment would be justified by need—not by profit.

Separation of the Diagnostic and Therapeutic Arms of Medicine

Consider a case of a physician who performs diagnostic and therapeutic procedures. This physician:

- Recommends a test be administered
- Performs the test on his equipment
- Executes and personally performs a procedure as a result of this test
- Judges the quality of the procedure
- Performs all follow-up on that procedure.

For each of these steps, the same physician is compensated. This type of situation could obviously lead to conflict of interest and abuse.

Again, let us emphasize that we are not talking of the family practitioner who may perform a small office procedure. We are talking about big-ticket items involving, for example, the decision to stop medical management and intervene mechanically in heart disease where the decision to intervene is often a subjective one based on interpretation of symptoms, degree of artery blockage, and amount of heart muscle at risk.

In addition, in the United States today, it is presently considered good and ethical practice in cardiology for the cardiologist to:

- Evaluate a patient
- Recommend a stress test (on their equipment)
- Recommend a heart catheterization
- Perform the heart catheterization

- Recommend a therapeutic balloon angioplasty
- Perform the balloon angioplasty
- Perform long-term follow-up.

For each of these steps, compensation is received.

We suggest that the cardiologist do the diagnostics, including the stress test, and have no problem with the cardiologist owning the "small-ticket" items such as a treadmill. The cardiologist, based on that, may recommend and perform a heart catheterization. The cardiologist should not own the catheterization laboratory equipment. If a therapeutic decision must be made for mechanical intervention, as opposed to continued medical therapy, at that point the cardiologist should refer the patient either to a cardiologist angioplasty specialist (who would in no way be financially connected with the diagnostic cardiologist), or to a cardiac surgeon for coronary artery bypass.

The diagnostic cardiologist should not benefit financially from the decision to intervene. Once the patient had the procedure—balloon angioplasty or atherectomy or coronary bypass—we would suggest that the patient be returned to the original diagnostic cardiologist. He would then re-evaluate the patient and be responsible for judging the results of the procedure that was performed and do the follow-up. This would reduce the incentive to do too much.

Until such reforms are made in the system, your best protection is to choose a physician of integrity. Your secondary defense must be knowledgeable third-party case management. Insurance funds should not be paid to physicians "in the dark." Different philosophies are allowed in medicine, but there are standard indications for most procedures. The installation of knowledgeable case managers to supervise the authorization for funding of medical care is an important protection for the health care consumer.

Fee-For-Service Insurance Costs Too Much

Fee-for-service insurance is too costly. This is the bottom line, and the "beast to be slain." If this type of policy were not too costly, we would all buy it.

Two factors have driven up the cost of fee-for-service insurance and deserve separate attention. These are Alternative Health Care Plans and cost shifting within hospitals.

Alternative Health Care Plans

Alternative Health Care plans, such as the various types of HMOs, have entered the health care arena and have sought to enroll only good risk patients. This leaves all the sick patients to buy fee-for-service insurance. The logic is very simple. If you take all the healthy people and put them in a separate health care delivery vehicle, their care will be very cheap. Their premiums can be low. However, if you leave only the sick people in the private insurance pool, the cost of taking care of those people will be extremely high. The solution here is fair and simple. Alternative plans must be made to accept all risk groups across the board, and they should be allowed to compete freely. So long as they accept their fair share of the elderly and the frail, these alternative health care plans deserve our blessing. Alternative care plans must accept their fair share of sick patients.

Cost Shifting within Hospitals

Private hospitals must break even or else they will be bankrupt. All hospitals lose money on Medicaid patients. In 1992, the majority of hospitals will lose money on Medicare patients. It is a common illusion that all private or self-paying patients receive the same rates from hospitals. This is simply that—an illusion. Many HMOs and even private carriers have negotiated favorable rates with their hospitals in return for referring all of their patients. The losses from Medicare and Medicaid and the losses on special contracts must all be made up to keep the hospital from entering bankruptcy. This is done by transferring the losses to private fee-for-service patients. This practice is known as **cost shifting**. Not all patients in hospitals are equal. Many patients pay the hospital far less than the cost of the care they receive. Others face astronomical bills. Why? Because they must pay not only for themselves, but also for those who generate a loss and they must also provide the private hospital with a profit to reinvest in its business.

Here is an example of this privileged carrier status. In one of our states, a very large private insurance carrier administers Medicare and Medicaid for the federal government and the state. The same private carrier has many privately insured patients. This company reimburses hospitals and doctors for their private patients on a system similar to the Medicare system but at a rate lower than the other health care plans pay. Other private health plans in the state find themselves subsidizing this large carrier. Does your health plan and your insurance company subsidize another large private insurance company? Do you want to?

Corporate America cannot control governmental funding of Medicare and Medicaid. The money is simply not there. The poor and indigent need health care too. However, there is something that corporate America and the private insurance plans can do. They can negotiate contracts with their hospitals to guarantee that their patients will receive the most favorable rates granted to any other private sector patient. This will not eliminate cost shifting or prevent providing care. It will guarantee that all nongovernmental plans will be treated equally because health care costs for the poor will be equally shared by all private carriers.

Summary

A health care plan that pays for care as you need it and makes available expensive specialist consultation and treatment is clearly the best system. Fee-for-service plans, once the most common in the market place, are becoming less available as they are made too expensive by cost shifting. People with these plans subsidize all the shortfalls from others in less desirable plans. There are some drawbacks to the fee-for-service system, but with vigilance and safeguards, this is the recommended plan. (The authors purchase it for themselves and their families.)

Can we make the good old free enterprise, fee-for-service, system less costly? The answer is a resounding "yes." First, we must educate those covered in private fee-for-service plans so that they will recognize and value the cost of their health care. This education can be carried out by teaching employees the cost of medical care. Making employees pay for part of their health care will also teach them its value. Cafeteria plans encourage the health care consumer to use benefits wisely. Education is the best weapon against over utilization. Next, the cost can be controlled by selecting good doctors and by using knowledgeable third-party case managers to avoid the tendency to do too much.

Chapter 13

Payment Reform in the Health Care System

A Look at Legislation, but First, a Parable:

The laborers felt that they were being underpaid. They worked hard from morning to night. Though they had less skill-enhancing training than the plumbers, certainly their labor was more difficult than that of the more highly paid craftsmen. The laborers felt they deserved as much as the plumbers. The bricklayers argued that their work required as much skill-enhancing training time as the plumbers, but the intensity of their work in carrying and laying bricks was equally as hard as the laborers'. The bricklayers felt they should be paid more than the plumbers and the laborers.

The plumbers dissented because their trade was not only difficult, but it also involved exposing themselves to the risk of communicable disease from excrement and waste that were not a hazard to the bricklayers and laborers.

It was hard to put a price on the risk. The electricians jumped on the bandwagon—one mistake for them could result in sudden death.

No more, said the ironworkers, than we who clamber across beams high above the skyline. All, however, envied the steelworkers who worked for the big companies, for these workers made more than any and had great benefits.

The government realized that the total cost of labor was a high portion of the gross national product and was concerned that all be paid fairly. The government commissioned a study with representatives of ironworkers, steelworkers, laborers, bricklayers, electricians, and plumbers. All the trades met to analyze how much skill-enhancing time was necessary to enter each trade. Studies were done on how much each type of brick weighed and how many could be laid in a day and over what distance they were usually moved. How many electricians actually died of electrocution and how many plumbers caught infectious diseases from plying their trade?

The plumbers and steamfitters, who both worked with pipe, were asked how hard it was to run a one-hundred-foot length of pipe with seven elbows compared to putting in a boiler or draining a cesspool. Values were placed on each task. Gradually, an equation was formulated wherein the government computed the exact value of each man's time and labor.

The original representative of the steelworkers, seeing that all other trades envied the steelworkers, walked out. The representative knew that jealously would provoke undervaluing of the steelworkers' labor. However, the prestige and power of being on the commission was used to quickly attract another steelworker to take his place.

All factors were included in the final equation: stress, longevity, intensity of labor, skill levels necessary, and danger involved. Finally, the government decreed exactly how much each person would be paid. The laborers got a large pay raise; the steelworkers took a large cut; the plumbers and steamfitters stayed about the same; but the electricians received a moderate raise. Surprisingly, the danger the ironworkers faced was not seen to be as great as they felt it was, nor was much skill necessary to rivet beams, so they were cut back severely.

This new government plan was submitted to each group for analysis and consent. The laborers and electricians heartily endorsed the plan; the plumbers and steamfitters were relatively indifferent. The steelworkers and the ironworkers strongly opposed the plan, and they worried about long-term mortgage payments and negative change in lifestyle to be imposed on their families by the new government plan.

The AFL/CIO was thrown into strife. Some unions were strongly for and some strongly against the plan. It was steelworker against laborer. Electrician against ironworker. The unions fought until organized labor disintegrated.

Governmental price controls replaced the free market. Free enterprise had fallen to a system of socialistic, governmentally imposed wage levels. Now, all were equal. Each person knew exactly what an hour of their time was worth. The incentive to excel for greater gain, to innovate, and to be more productive were removed. Gradually, the quality of labor declined and the nation had difficulty competing in the world markets. The once great nation found itself a follower instead of a leader in industry and production. A once proud people witnessed another step in the decline of their society.

A Parallel

The United States is a leader of the world in the care and treatment of the seriously ill. We are the leader in the development of medical technology, from sophisticated magnetic resonance scanners to ingenious interarterial "roto-rooter" to remove life-threatening blockages in a patient's blood supply. We have inequities in payments among physicians. All seem to make a living, but there are disparities. Neonatologist (specialists in newborns) and pediatricians render service of inestimable value to our infants and children, but infants and children have no money, and parents tend to have infants and children while they are young and least likely to have health insurance or high paying jobs. Neonatologists and pediatricians are relatively underpaid.

The family practitioner is the cog by which the wheel turns—screening all, treating most routine illnesses, and acting as the "signpost" physician by which patients with complex illnesses are referred to the needed specialist. They toil long hours and have not had a salary increase in some time due to the cost control forces in medicine. The internist, the diagnostician, can see relatively few patients because each case is analyzed in depth. The internist prescribes the medical treatment for patients with more complex problems. He feels that he should receive greater compensation for each case than the family practitioner. He works the same long hours but cannot see as many patients.

The cardiologists (medical heart specialists) are highly compensated because they not only treat medical heart ailments, but they also do expensive heart catheterizations necessary to diagnose complex illness, and they treat some forms of coronary artery disease nonoperatively with the balloon or "roto-rooter."

Neurosurgeons, cardiac surgeons, eye surgeons, and plastic surgeons are all very highly compensated specialists whose work, to some, seems rather mechanical (i.e., non-cerebral) and therefore are felt to be overcompensated.

In its wisdom, the United States government decided to correct the inequities of the free market system and spent $2.5 million to determine exactly how much each person's labor was worth. The commission studied all factors—years of education, skill levels, stress involved, and time necessary to perform each task. An exact equation was drawn to determine precisely how much each physician should be paid for each task. The new system recommended large increases in compensation to the pediatricians, family practitioners, and diagnosticians, and large compensation cuts for the specialists in surgery.

The proposal was then sent down to each group. The American College of Family Practitioners endorsed the plan, The American College of Physicians endorsed the plan, and the American College of Surgeons condemned the plan. The American Medical Association was torn by its member groups and is seeking to prevent the disintegration of medicine as a whole. We could argue that as our population ages, many of the patients that surgeons treat are critically ill. Critically ill patients require more than mechanical skills of the surgeons and keep them up many sleepless nights in getting their patients through the postoperative period. We could argue that surgeons periodically get cut or stuck in surgery, exposing them to debilitating and lethal blood-borne diseases—hepatitis, AIDS. We could argue that the system takes no account of liability exposure. A specialty surgeon may pay over $100,000, whereas an internist may pay $3,000 for the same amount of malpractice insurance in the same area. This is a huge difference in the cost of doing business. We can argue that the internist should be higher paid per patient because he can see but few. We can argue that pediatricians render a service that can never be repaid, and it is tragic that the families who receive their services lack the means to pay them on the same scale that other physicians receive payment.

Let's forget all that. Let's look at two things: physician salaries and the new government-commissioned payment proposal, the **Harvard Resource Based Relative Value Scale** (HRBRVS) or so called "payment reform."

A review of physician salaries shows the majority of American physicians are relatively well paid. Those who live in poverty generally do so because of decisions they consciously make to deliver care to the needy under courageous circumstances. As in all aspects of life, some do better than others. Over the last decade, physician salaries have not gone up. A recent study showed average physicians actually earn 10 percent less now than they did in 1980. Inflation has slowed, but is constant, causing a relative decrease in buying power of 40 percent to the average physician. The cost of physician care in the same period has markedly increased because of increased utilization of physicians by our population. The result is that physician costs are up but the individual physician earns *less*. Few Americans, rich or poor, have seen a 40-50 percent erosion in earning power over the last decade. It is unnecessary to cut physician salaries. If we simply leave them where they are, soon they will be "poor like us." Now the question is, do we want physicians who are "poor like us"?

As physicians have become relatively poorer and the liability climate deteriorates, the number of applicants to medical schools has dropped. Consider:

- In 1973, there were 42,000 applicants for 13,000 positions.
- In 1981, there were 35,000 applicants for 15,000 positions.
- In 1987, there were 28,000 applicants for 15,000 positions. (See Figure 13.1.)

Quoting from the *New York Times*, August 14, 1988: Dr. Martin Kervis, Vice Dean of the University of Illinois College of Medicine, "To fill their classes, the colleges of medicine must dig deeper and deeper into the applicant pool." The last ten years has seen the grade average of entrants drop to the point that some schools now consider cutting back slots rather than see standards fall to unacceptable levels. In short, as return on investment drops, fewer of our most talented youth seek entrance to the medical field. The 75-year-olds in our society will not be hurt by this trend. The 40-year-old will.

As this book goes to press, we see confusion in how the RBRVS or prospective payment reform will be administered. The government has used the proposed system of price controls in medicine in an attempt to cut costs of care—attempting to cut the cost of high-priced specialists without increasing reimbursement to the under-paid practitioners. Politicians are using a totally untried theoretical mathematical model not to distribute financial reward more fairly than the free market but to cut costs.

Figure 13.1   Medical School Applicants

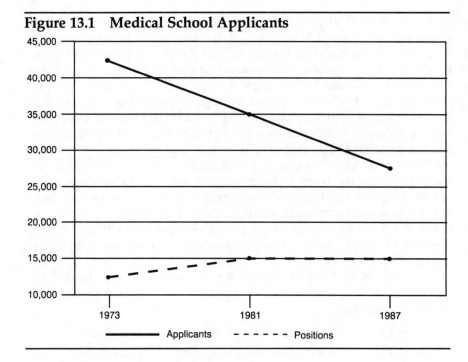

Tax what you would be rid of and subsidize what you would have grow. This will lead to availability of medical services based on political discussion rather than on medical need. As inequities in the system become manifest, the availability of certain services will be threatened.

The second point of analysis is the concept of governmental price fixing in medicine using the RBRVS equation that determines the worth of each person's time. In other fields, government price fixing has simply not worked. Rent control is a primary example. Initially, housing is artificially cheap but without a profit motive, no new housing becomes available and ultimately the consumer pays the price.

The ultimate example of governmental price control is in Cairo where, one hundred years ago, the government fixed the price so that the poor could have affordable rent. With no profit, the landlords could not fix their buildings so that now we have the "city of the dead" dwellers. They live and raise their families in the tombs of the rich people in the cemetery because they are in better condition than the apartments that the landlords cannot afford to repair. The implementation of wage and price controls has always led to economic downturns and recession.

As the government enters the free marketplace and determines how much any profession is worth, we open the door for government to define the worth of *all* in the free marketplace. How much should CEOs be paid? What is their time worth? Can American industry be made more efficient by controlling the wages of management? Will this make our manufacturing segment more competitive in the world market? Can the government do this by determining how much each worker's time is worth and adjusting their salary accordingly?

In totalitarian Eastern Block nations with government-managed economies, artificial government-controlled pricing has led to years of economic stagnation leading to the total inability of those nations to compete with the West in standard of living. Recently, the whole thrust of "perestroika" has been a return to free market values.

We set a dangerous precedent in a free market society when we allow the government to determine values of goods and services in the private sector. For now, we look at physician fees, but legal costs in our society have outpaced inflation in medical care. How much may an attorney make?

What about wage pressures in automobile workers (if we have any American automobile workers left)? The price of automobiles in the United States has climbed faster than the cost of health care. Are excess benefits making corporate America less competitive? Or, who has the right to determine what benefits an employee should have? A dollar mandated to health care or any other benefit is a dollar taken from somewhere else. Shall the government mandate our health care coverage? If a person has saved his money and wants a health care service not covered under a government program, should he or she have the right to pay for it and obtain it? Will it exist? Does this mean a two-tier system, one for the rich and one for the poor? We have all seen the Soviet Union disintegrate as a result of 74 years of bureaucratic governmental control of goods and services. Russian and Eastern European political leaders now have their future and the future of their countries based on increasing productivity through the stimulus of the free market. In the West, we are turning to governmental price controls to tinker with the finest system of health care in the world. It is a dangerous precedent to invite governmental wage and price controls into the free market, even if we do it one sector at a time.

Chapter 14

Liability in Medicine

Has the "God Complex" returned to haunt doctors? Everyone expects a perfect result. Does a bad result mean a bad doctor? If a severely retarded baby is born, should that baby's lifelong care be financed from the savings of the aging obstetrician who had the misfortune to deliver the child?

The liability problem is difficult to discuss because the extent of the liability crisis is determined by state law. There are 50 states. Therefore, we do not have one problem; we have 50 problems.

Arizona Backlog

Sunday, February 19, 1989, the *Arizona Republic* proclaimed in front page headlines "Physician Complaints Backlogged." "The Arizona Board of Medical examiners is choking on a growing backlog of cases, forcing delays of months or even years in litigating complaints against some of the state's 6,400 doctors." The number of doctors being investigated by the Board of litigation jumped from 56 in 1987 to 1,010 in 1988, or about 16 percent of the state's doctors—in a single year—in Arizona!

Doctors vary in competence, but it is a very rare doctor that would deliberately harm a patient. When litigation is in the offing against 16 percent of Arizona's doctors in a single year, either Arizona medicine is saddled with the biggest bunch of bozos since the Ringling Brothers, or else there is something drastically wrong with our system of litigation.

Has court action become the American way to settle disputes? America has 5 percent of the world's population, 70 percent of the world's attorneys, and 96 percent of the world's litigation.

The Cost of the Liability Crisis

The average U.S. physician pays 5 percent of gross revenues for liability insurance. Thoracic surgeons, neurosurgeons, and obstetricians pay over 10 percent of their gross revenues. In some states, a cardiac surgeon's malpractice premium is in excess of $1,000 per open heart surgery performed. If you or your corporation buys health care in a high liability state, you cannot afford to be uninterested. The most conservative estimates indicate that the overall cost of health care could be reduced by 25 to 35 percent if the liability problem were solved.

Liability and the Quality of Medicine

Does malpractice action raise the quality of medicine? There is *no* evidence that incompetent physicians are more likely to be sued than competent ones. Do you live in a high liability state? Let me tell you a story.

Two years ago, we had 19 obstetricians in our town. As liability claims mounted, and insurance became less affordable, the older physicians retired. One middle-aged individual joined a drug company to do research for a salary. Several younger obstetricians moved to a neighboring state where reimbursement for procedures was 30 percent higher and cost of liability insurance was 87 percent lower.

The women in our town continued having babies at the same rate, even though we had 33 percent fewer obstetricians. We have a very nice town in which to live. Our economy is stable. Our crime rate is low. We have an excellent symphony, a wonderful education system, and diversified industry. But we needed more obstetricians.

We knew that over 50 percent of all doctors will practice within a 50-mile radius of the site where they completed residency. With this information, we went to the best obstetrics training program in the state only to discover that rather than staying within a 50-mile radius, over 80 percent of all graduating trainees left our state.

If you were a bright, competent physician who could go anywhere and be successful, would you choose a high liability climate in which to practice? Do you think the high liability atmosphere would increase the probability of recruiting physicians who, for reasons of personality, education, or other reasons, would have a harder time getting a position elsewhere? Does this mean that the high costs of liability judgements in our state may not only have economic repercussions, but also could seriously reduce the level of care available to child-bearing women. Will the liability crisis adversely affect the level of care to be received by you, or your family?

Origin of the Problem: Thank You Professor Priest

The liability crisis in the United States threatens the productivity of our industry, destroys research and development in our society, and sucks the life's blood from our health care system. To understand how our code of civil law came to be so distorted, we lean on the work of Professor George Priest of Yale University Law School who has eloquently outlined the historical development of the problem.

The function of civil law in the United States is continuously evolving. In its most primitive form, law served to protect the property rights of man and society. From here, contract law evolved to uphold the value of the promise of one interacting agent with another, otherwise known as contractual agreements, either written or spoken. Finally, liability law was developed to compensate individuals and society for injury sustained when a person or agent, acting contrary to the social norm of fitting behavior, inflicted such damage. Such was the working concept of our legal code up until the 1960s. In this era, the concept of negligence of culpability was central in establishing the defendant's responsibility for an injury and his or her obligation to provide recompense to the plaintiff. To be found guilty and liable, the defendant had to do something wrong and had to act in some way outside of and antagonistic to the good of society.

In the 1960s, the concept of liability and damage was completely transformed not by legislative statute or popular vote, but by the judicial acceptance of the proposition that liability judgements should allocate the cost of civil damages not to those who cause them *but to those best able to pay*. This proposition does not consider negligence as a necessary element. Since every action of human beings has potential for benefit and harm, under this doctrine every human action, no matter how well intentioned or with whatever forethought, may be subject to a negative liability judgement. The individual who acts completely within the law and with good intent is no longer protected from legal responsibility for their actions, even if that harm was impossible to foresee. In a landmark verdict in 1982, the New Jersey Supreme Court ruled in *Beshoda vs. John Mansville* that the asbestos manufacturer was liable for a cancer in a worker even though the cancer occurred before it was known that asbestos caused cancer. The defense argued that at the time of the injury there was no scientific proof linking asbestos with cancer; therefore, the Mansville Corporation was not liable. Plaintiff's counsel argued that this defense was irrelevant.

The court concurred holding that the manufacturer was liable for breaching its duty to warn the worker that asbestos causes cancer, though the court accepted that at the time of the breach it was impossible scientifically to have known that asbestos causes cancer. (George L. Priest, the new Legal Structure of Risk Control, Daedalus, Vol. 119 #4, pg. 218)

Liability for an action impossible to prevent is a difficult concept. Most reasonable people think of liability in context of damages resulting from violation of some moral or legislative standard. Liability for unavoidable acts is fully in accord with the new doctrine that every action is capable of harm and if harm occurs its costs should be internalized to the perpetrators. In fact, acceptance of this concept transforms liability law into a form of insurance. An action that cannot be prevented can only be insured against. In theory then, this concept would take the place of first-party insurance by internalizing the cost of injury to those involved in the injury and allocating the cost of the injury to those most able to pay—without respect to negligence.

Under this utilitarian social doctrine, two principles of the law will apply. First, if an injury could be prevented, liability will be adjudicated to the party in the best relative position to have prevented it. Second, if an injury could not have been prevented, liability will be assigned to the party best able to spread the risks. Let's look at these two principles with some examples:

First, if an injury could have been prevented, liability will be assigned to the party in the best relative position to have prevented it.

With respect to this principle, the courts often make some assumptions:

- Cities have more control than citizens over risk in public areas.
- Manufacturers have more control over product safety than consumers.
- Hospitals and physicians have more control over the outcome of procedures than patients.

Limiting ourselves to the malpractice area, it might be asked if hospitals and physicians have more control over the outcome of procedures than the disease process itself?

An obstetrician might give his life totally to the practice of medicine. He might identify with a birthing child. He may grieve with the parents at an ill-born's defects, but if a court determines the risk of injury was within the control of the physician through any act, omission, or technical judgement, or that the insurance of the physician was in the best position to spread injury costs, the liability for a lifetime of losses may be assigned to him. In this way, the cost of caring for the child is shifted from parents and state to the obstetrician. The result is that 15 percent of obstetricians have given up delivering babies. More physicians are refusing certain types of cases because of increased risks of liability.

The second principle of modern liability practices is harder to fathom. It states that if an injury could not be prevented, liability will be assigned to the party best able to spread the risk. Here the law deviates from a safety net function to an insurance function. In the business sector, large companies and small family businesses will be held accountable for unforeseeable injury that they had no control to prevent. In medicine, a physician's liability premium and personal assets may be used as a form of social security payments for injuries over which there is no control. For example, years ago, infants born with premature lungs died at birth. It was discovered that placing these children in an incubator or 100 percent oxygen could save some of them. Later, it was discovered that 100 percent oxygen could cause blindness in newborns. Now, we have children who otherwise would have been dead suing the physician who saved their lives for damage to their eyes. The court accepts that there was no way for the physician to know that the lifesaving procedure caused blindness, yet average court awards against physicians exceed three million dollars per case under this doctrine of spreading the risk.

These two principles have changed litigation from disputes between individuals to judicial mandates with the intent to maximize the
welfare of the society. Under older principles, a farmer who pre-sold
grain to a dealer but could not deliver because of drought would be
liable. Today, it might be argued that the farmer had no control over
the drought but the dealer could have minimized the injury by contract-
ing with farmers in diversified locations. Thus, the burden of liability
might be laid upon the dealer.

Liability today is seen as a form of secondary insurance for injury
for the less well off and those in least positions to afford primary insurance. Does this serve the highest good of society?

In the manufacturing sector, many products have been taken off
the market and many research and development projects discontinued
for fear of sustaining liability. This costs us jobs at home and makes us
less competitive abroad. As an example, the American General Aviation
Industry, which manufactured 18,000 planes a year in its heyday, is
now almost nonexistent and manufactures about 1,000 planes a year because of the enormous cost of liability.

In medicine, women may have difficulty finding a board-certified
skilled obstetrician in some areas of the country because liability fears
have driven physicians from the field. Many physicians are reluctant to
care for trauma and emergency cases because they may be deemed in
best position to "spread the risk" of bearing the cost of injuries over
which they have no control.

From a social standpoint, many communities have begun to restrict
or no longer offer some services because of liability risk. Playground
equipment has been removed from some public playgrounds; diving
boards removed from some public pools; and some wildlife areas previously open to the public have been closed.

From an economic standpoint, "tort law" insurance is much cost-
lier to society than is first-party insurance. For instance, it is estimated
that similar claims will be requited with two to three times the reimbursement under "tort law" than they would be under first-party insurance. In addition, the cost of administering "tort law insurance"
through the court system is conservatively estimated at five to ten times
the cost of underwriting first-party insurance. In fact, tort law insurance
is in fact a regressive tax on the poor and least well off members of
society. The American system of taxation has long been a progressive
one (i.e., the highest income members of our society are asked to pay a

progressively increasing percentage of the tax burden while the middle class pays a lower share percentage-wise and the very poor are exempt). "Tort Law Insurance" forces manufacturers, service companies, and physicians to pro-rate their liability costs into the cost of their products. To purchase a product or service, a poor person bears the same premium as a rich person. Furthermore, if a poor person suffers injury from a manufactured product or medical service, the courts will take into account earning potential lost when calculating an award.

What we have done then is set up an extremely costly secondary insurance system that is effectively forcing the removal of many goods and services from our society, driving up the cost of medical care, and perhaps forcing rationing of medical care. We finance this expensive system internally by raising the cost of goods and services that may be subject to liability. This cost is then borne equally by the poor and rich alike who purchase these goods or services. Again, though the poor person pays the same premium if they are injured, their award will be less than that of the rich person because their potential lost income will be calculated as less.

It is time to reform the tort system of this country to its purpose to recompense those injured through negligence or a breach of standard behavior. The tort system was never meant to provide social insurance to compensate for acts of God, nature, and the nature of the disease process. The present philosophy of tort law decreases the competitiveness of our industry in the world and drains badly needed dollars from our already stressed local government and health care systems. We need a tough, efficient economical tort system that will grant fair access and fair, but not excessive, awards to those who are truly injured. We need a tort system that sees to it that the lion's share of awards go to the injured—not to attorney and court costs. We believe that this is possible with a healthy change of philosophy and the implementation of tort reform.

Doctors Must Be Protected from Lawsuits when They Are Appointed to Police Other Doctors

Under the guidance of state law, hospitals have introduced **Quality Assurance** (Q.A.) **Committees**. These committees are set up to protect you. Whenever a patient dies or has a bad outcome, that patient's case in reviewed behind closed doors by the Q.A. panel doctors. Their job is to assure that you had good treatment. Presently, many physicians who serve on Q.A. panels are afraid that they will be sued if they censure or remove privileges from an incompetent colleague.

Recently, the United States Supreme Court rendered a decision in *Patrick vs. Burgett* that bankrupted many of the physicians on a quality assurance committee that censured a colleague. Now, this is not the clearest case, since some of the censuring physicians may have acted from less than noble motives. But who will judge their motives? It is well-known in medical circles that good doctors get sued just like bad doctors. Physicians are not attorneys. Those who function to protect the medical consumer in reviewing the actions of another doctor are never certain when they may be sued. Physicians appointed to police other doctors by serving on Quality Assurance committees have no protection through their malpractice insurance. Liability insurance protects only for malpractice. It does not protect a doctor from being sued for slander or antitrust when he or she censures a colleague. If the hospital accepts responsibility for the action of its physicians, then it, too, may be directly liable.

In *Patrick vs. Burgett*, the doctors were found personally liable. Many of them came to financial ruin. Some legal experts feel that physicians will be protected for quality assurance work if their intentions are good. Who is to pass judgement on their intentions? Even if their intentions are the best, how do we know a jury will see them as such?

Report Bad Doctors

All claims should be reported so that bad doctors can be traced. Until recently, substandard physicians were able to practice in one locale until they generated so many problems that they were either invited to leave or until they decided to do so on their own. They moved to the next town, again setting up practice, to create more problems. This is possible because claims against physicians and censures against physicians were carried out on an in-state basis. Since each state licenses physicians individually, a bad doctor could move from state A to state B, apply once again for malpractice insurance, and set up practice to create more harm. This was an intolerable situation, and the authors supported legislation to set up a nationwide computer system so that all claims against physicians could be reported. Physicians' records now follow them and are available to any state licensing board to which the physician might apply. To protect the physician/victim of inappropriate litigation from a lifetime burden, we recommend amending the act so that all claims would be removed from the record after five years.

Confine Physician Liability to Malpractice

True victims of malpractice should be compensated for their economic loss. Malpractice should be recoverable from the physician's liability policy. The award should be fair and just.

A Bad Result Is NOT the Same as Malpractice

Bad results do not equal malpractice. Five percent of all babies will have birth defects. Only a small percentage of these will in any way reflect the care of the obstetrician who delivered the baby. Bad results should be compensated under the social welfare system, not under the physician's liability insurance. Despite claims to the contrary, your doctor is not God. He or she cannot cure all ills. There is pain and suffering and incurable disability in life. We must face that fact if we are to retain a system that will provide us with quality health care in our time of need.

Impose Moderate but Fair Caps on Pain and Suffering

The principle that guides liability should be punishment or elimination of incompetent physicians, not financial rewards for the victims. If my child were killed, I would know indescribable pain. No amount of money would bring back my child or eliminate that pain. If my child were killed because of a physician whose **pattern of practice is incompetent**, that physician should not be allowed to practice.

Pain is a part of the human condition. We go through life facing physical and emotional hardship. Who deserves pay for pain more—the disabled victim of an automobile accident or the disabled soldier who survives after five years of torture in a POW camp? To which of these does our society give more? If our society has money to pay out for pain, maybe we should locate and pay the remaining survivors of Auschwitz. What is this concept that our society pays for the pain aspect of illness with money—money that drives the costs of our health care system up?

It Pays to Advertise

It has been said that attorneys tend to sue those with money because they do better. Take a patient who is in an accident and suffers a badly fractured leg. He goes to an orthopedist and despite appropriate treatment, the fracture doesn't heal well. The leg is deformed. The jury must keep in mind that the treating orthopedist did not fracture the leg. Perhaps responsibility for the residual deformity lies with the uninsured truck that ran over the leg, not the insured orthopedist who tried to fix it.

Should a hospital that is scrupulous in credentialing its physicians and has set up quality assurance procedures be held liable if one of its physicians makes a mistake? Lawsuits must be confined to the party who committed the injustice, *not* extended to the bystander with money.

Punitive Damages Should Seldom Be Awarded in Personal Injury Suits

Punitive damages (those damages awarded a victim over and above compensation for actual loss, to punish the perpetrator of the deed) should be reserved to the rare doctor who actually sought to do harm to his patient. Some doctors may chase the buck. They all have different skill levels. But not many of them go into practice to hurt human beings. Punitive awards in medical cases are rare in Canada and other countries; they should be rare in the United States, too.

Limit Contingency Fees for Attorneys

One New York firm received $11 million in contingency fees in a single year for malpractice liability cases. One attorney in Washington, D.C. billed over $5 million in medical malpractice fees in a single year. The contingency fee system has been touted as a unique facet of American law that allows the poor equal access to justice. Through custom and attorney advertising—"Injured, call us. It won't cost you anything unless we collect"—it has been perverted into an ill-conceived lottery system for anyone who alleges injury. Unfortunately, 30 to 50 percent of the truly injured person's award goes to the uninjured attorney, while a portion of the rest must go for expert witnesses and expenses. Often *less* than half is paid out to the plaintiff. The authors feel that contingency fees above expenses should be capped so that more of any award would go to the aggrieved. This would also lessen the incentive for un-scrupulous attorneys to seek unreasonable compensation.

Eliminate Fee Splitting Among Attorneys

If a family physician refers a patient to a specialist for a procedure, it is considered unethical for him or her to receive any money in return for that referral. People feel receiving money for such a referral would en-courage family physicians to send too many people for unneeded pro-cedures.

In law, if a family attorney refers a client to a specialist litigator, he or she may receive a fee or a percentage of the award. Don't people feel that receiving money for such a referral would encourage local attor-neys to send too many people for unneeded lawsuits? Why is "fee split-ting" considered unethical for physicians but ethical for attorneys? Shouldn't physicians and attorneys, as professional people of honor, face the same ethical standards? In our country, paying money to some-one who gives you a job or a contract is known as a "bribe." It is pun-ishable by jail. It is not right in industry. It is not right in medicine. Why should this be considered ethical practice for attorneys?

Discourage Marginal and Frivolous Lawsuits: Make the Loser Pay Court Costs

Eight out of ten malpractice actions are decided in favor of the physician. But even the most righteous physicians, if sued, will spend many sleepless nights worrying what their fate will be before a jury of their peers. Even when found innocent, the emotional and economic cost of surviving the battle is high. Our society does not repay the innocent person for the pain they felt while going through the trial. You, the consumer of health care, *must pay* the economic cost by bearing your share of the physi-cian's malpractice premium. Why not make those who create these costs, by suing the innocent person, pay the costs that they have in-jected into the system?

Suspend Medical Licenses

Physicians are human. All humans are fallible. We do not wish to injure or remove the competent, conscientious physicians. They devote their lives to their patients; but like all other human beings, they are capable of making a mistake. We wish to identify and remove from practice those physicians whose pattern of practice demonstrates incompetence and who bring harm to patients.

Punish the bad doctors. Do not reward misery. Suspend medical licenses of people who are incapable of the practice of good medicine. Society cannot tolerate incompetence simply because they have an academic degree. The object of liability reform is to get rid of bad doctors, not to bankrupt medicine and corporate America.

The liability crisis must not be allowed to destroy the system that provides medical care for all of us. Our medical system was developed to provide quality health care to the sick, not to provide a lottery for the injured and a retirement plan for attorneys.

Chapter 15

Some Solutions

There is money in our society to care for our sick if we spend it wisely. We have the finest system for patient care in history. Our technology is responsible for the most advanced diagnostic and therapeutic breakthroughs in the world. We have technology and scientific tools that other democracies with socialized medicine cannot afford. We may be the unusual industrialized nation with private sector health care, but we are also the technological engine that provides tomorrow's diagnostic and therapeutic tools for the rest of the world. To dismantle this free enterprise driven program hurts not only our children, but also for all of humanity.

To save our health care delivery system and make it better, we must do certain things. These are divided into:

- **Immediate steps**—the things to do today
- **Intermediate steps**—the things to strive for in the near future
- **Long-term goals**—things that we must use our influence to have society bring about.

Immediate Steps

1. Choose your personal or corporate physician team wisely. Competent physicians tend to refer patients to other competent physicians. Incompetent physicians often feel insecure. They worry about losing their patients. Often times, they are reluctant to refer their patients to a good physician because they are afraid the patients won't return.
   Physicians with integrity are your best protection against unnecessary testing, unnecessary procedures, unnecessary hospitalizations, and unecessary services that sell you too much health care no matter what the system.
   Physicians with integrity are your best protection against a less than optimal health care delivery vehicle. Physicians who dedicate their lives to medicine and the care of their patients will make any sacrifice to see that those patients receive the care that they need.

2. Choose the best health care delivery vehicle you can afford. Do comparison shopping. See what each plan costs; see what each plan covers. Compare benefits carefully. Don't let yourself be frustrated in a time of need with inadequate coverage. Read the fine print.

3. If your corporation is large enough, **self-insure** with a third-party administrator (TPA). This eliminates the profit margins that insurance companies must have to survive.

If you control large numbers of patients, don't self-insure blindly. Sit down with your health care providers. Pick first-rate providers and then negotiate discounts in return for a promise to spend your health care dollars with them. Remember, at this moment health care premiums exceed health care costs by a huge margin. For now, self-insurance using negotiated payment plans with health care providers and knowledgeable third-party case management would seem the best direction to pursue.

A word on knowledgeable third-party case management. At the present time, this is often understood as scanning inpatient admissions. If the patient is in the hospital 11 days instead of 9 days, the manager calls the physician to find out why the average length of stay has been exceeded. This type of approach to third-party case management can use up your case manager's time and your physician's goodwill. It can engender hostility on the part of both the health care providers and health care consumers. Perhaps the major part of your case manager's time should be spent in **accrediting** the doctors who will serve your plan. Perhaps the best way to manage the cases is to check the **credentials** of the doctors who provide care. Consider:

- What is their track record?
- How many cases do they handle?
- Of all patients who come through their office, what percentage go on to have specialized tests and procedures compared to the percentage of the normal population?
- What is the usual cost of managing each type of case by physician?
- What is the usual length of hospitalization?
- Outcome analysis—if a physician or group of physicians treats a population of patients, how does that population do in the long-term outcome when compared to other groups of patients with similar problems being treated in the area, the region, the country?

Human beings are biological organisms. They do not always read the book. They do not always follow the rules. Review a physician's credentials, overall level of practice, and billing pattern. This will protect the economics of your medical plan more than checking on an extra day's hospitalization under the care of a physician on whom your plan has no data.

Educate health plan participants to the cost and value of the health care that they receive. Most over-utilization of health care springs from ignorance. Plan participants do not realize the value and cost of the health care that they abuse to themselves, to their employers, and to society. Increased utilization is the single largest factor in driving up overall cost of medicine in the United States. Education is the remedy.

Education can be carried out through informative programs or one-on-one sessions. It also can be carried out in a practical way through increased coinsurance, increased deductibles, and increased premiums. Cafeteria plans provide useful tools in educating plan participants to the value of the care that they will receive. We must instill in health care consumers an appreciation of the value of the plan in which they are enrolled. They must appreciate the care that they are going to receive. They must feel responsibility and ownership of the plan. They must know that if the health care delivery systems in the United States collapse, it is their care that will be compromised or no longer available. We must instill in health care consumers the principle of careful purchasing of health care to protect their system. Health care consumers who are careful in their choice of a physician, who discuss the alternatives with respect to managing their illness, and who will educate themselves in the various ways of treating their illness may be the greatest tool that we have in controlling health care costs at the present time.

Intermediate Solutions

Physician Reform

Remove physicians from conflicts of interest. The public must learn to discern the difference between the physician groups who provide simple on-site blood testing and x-ray services for the convenience of their patients and those more aggressive groups who have purchased multimillion dollar CAT scanners, MRIs, and heart catheterization laboratories in communities where these same services might be otherwise available. Physicians who have ownership interest in major testing facilities in their community may have an inherent conflict of interest. They must keep utilization rates up to insure return on their investment. In communities where there is no other source of investment capital, society should overlook this conflict and allow physician ownership for the overall good. In most communities where other sources of capital are available, physicians should not be allowed to refer into self-owned multi-million dollar testing facilities. If these facilities are over-utilized, needed health care dollars will be drained from the community. American health care consumers must use common sense to determine what is reasonable. The family practitioner with simple testing equipment is reasonable. The 20-man group practice with more sophisticated x-ray and laboratory facilities on site is reasonable. The small group of physicians who set up a multi-million dollar magnetic resonance scanner and self-refer into it in competition with the other magnetic resonance scanner at the local hospital is unreasonable. Physicians should be allowed to own a sophisticated scanner to compete with their hospital only if they do not self-refer into their own facility.

Liability Reform

Conservative estimates indicate that the overall cost of medicine in the United States could be deceased by 25 to 35 percent if we could control the liability problem. Malpractice premiums which, if reduced, could decrease the cost of medicine by 5 percent are only a small part. Thirty percent of all tests ordered by physicians are felt to be part of the practice of so-called defensive medicine. As long as the system remains unchanged, the cost of medicine will be inflated tremendously by physicians' attempts to protect themselves and their families from disaster.

Reality

A single million dollar verdict takes funds that could screen 15,000 women for breast cancer, remove 1,000 documented lung cancers, or restore 300 young executives to the workplace after coronary bypass. Even when there is no verdict, how much of our resources are consumed by the cost of litigation? How many healthier babies would be born if that money were spent on prenatal care for the indigent?

The Need to Focus

The goal of liability reform is the improvement of quality through the elimination of bad doctors rather than perpetuating the current financial problems that threaten to eliminate quality medicine. We must have immunity for peer review, liability limited to malpractice, punitive awards limited to cases with mal-intent, fair caps on awards for pain and suffering, elimination of fee-splitting among attorneys, suspension of physicians with incompetent patterns of practice, and financial penalties for frivolous lawsuits.

Medicare Reforms

As the majority of hospitals lose money on Medicare patients, that financial loss is shifted to the private sector. This drives up the bill. However, there is a more sinister portion of the problem that we have not yet examined. That portion of the problem is what happens as Medicare goes bankrupt. At its present funding levels, Medicare is predicted to go bankrupt between 1994 and 2000, according to the annual report of the Board of Trustees of the Federal Hospital Insurance Fund. At the present time, 2.9 percent of the American citizen's income goes to the

Medicare Trust Fund. Under three out of four economic scenarios predicted by Federal Hospital Insurance Fund trustees, the cost of Medicare will exceed that 2.9 percent tax within the next three years. Once this occurs, several things can happen:

1. The promised benefits to our disabled and elderly can be reduced to control costs.
2. We can shift funds from the social security retirement fund to cover the difference.
3. We can increase taxes.
4. We can apply "means testing" for eligibility.

The implication of preserving Medicare delivery by increasing taxes must be clearly understood. First, as personal taxes go up, disposable income for working Americans will go down. This will lower the quality of life for people presently working. Second, as corporate taxes increase, there will be a decrease in reinvestment capital and a decrease in the ability of industry to compete in the world markets.

Third, if this alternative is chosen, it must be with the understanding that sacrifices on the part of the present workers and United States industry will benefit present retirees only. The money will not be there to give 40-year-old working Americans a similar level of care during their retirement. Our population is aging. In 20 years, there will simply not be enough young workers to pay for the level of health care that present retirees receive.

The problem originates in the "pay-as-you-go" funding system upon which our social welfare system and Medicare are based. Pay-as-you-go cannot function in a population that is aging. There were many more workers to share the health care of each disabled person and retiree in 1965 than there are now. In another 25 years, there may be less than two workers under the age of 65 to support the cost of health care for each person over the age of 65 and eligible for Medicare under the present standards.

The answer is reform by switching from pay-as-you-go to funding the system on a sound actuarial basis. This will protect both present and future generations. **Actuarial funding** means that money paid in would not all be spent on the health care needs of today. It would be invested at interest so that when you are retired or disabled that money can cover your health care.

Americans already on Medicare cannot be abandoned. We must continue to support them on a pay-as-you-go basis. We must establish a national "tax-incentive" system that encourages us to invest for our own future health care needs and potential long-term care requirements. This could be accomplished by allowing individuals to establish health care IRA accounts and long-term care accounts. This will insure quality health care when there are fewer young people to support the system. Gradual conversion of Medicare funding to a sound actuarial system will protect present and future generations.

Long-Term Solutions

Some long-term solutions include controlled downsizing and restoration of profitability.

Downsizing the System

There is not money to continue to support our system of health care at the present growth rate. Two alternative scenarios are possible in view of the necessity to control costs.

In the first scenario, the one that we see taking place around us today, the government and third-party payers simply cut back on cash inflow, thus allowing hospitals to close, allowing physician incomes to drop, and allowing the removal of capital from the system so that health care providers may no longer be able to purchase the new technology.

As physician quality of life declines, the number of qualified applicants per place in medical school will continue to fall. As the lot of the physician becomes unhappy and medical schools churn out more and more physicians of lower and lower quality, the new physician product, the new health care system, will be composed of less talent and less motivation. The overall standard of care will fall, the incentive to produce new technology will disappear, and the overall quality of the American medical system will disintegrate.

The second scenario, which we espouse, is called **controlled downsizing**. The key to controlled downsizing is the production of fewer physicians. Physicians should be allowed to earn a good living so that there will be an incentive for quality people to enter the profession. But, the overall cost of health care delivery should be controlled by limiting the overall number of health care providers. Would the poor suffer most in loss of medical care? Not necessarily. It would be simple, as part of medical school acceptance, to require an agreement to service in designated under-privileged areas for a fixed period of years before being allowed to practice in one's chosen environment. Every young physician, upon the completion of his or her training, would give a portion of their life to the poor and underprivileged. Once the designated time period was over, that physician could continue to practice in that environment or could move to another environment.

This system would involve some rationing of care, but all would share equally. It would provide care for the poor and the wealthy. It would allow the incentive for technological development to remain. Furthermore, as resources accumulated in the system through sound actuarial funding and elimination of excess, the number of high quality physician providers could be allowed to grow. Controlled downsizing would provide for equally shared rationing, maintenance of quality, and the capability of expansion at high quality levels when funding for that expansion becomes available.

Turning the System Profitable

The current crisis in medicine in the United States results in large part from over-utilization of a system that currently has a capacity to provide care at a greater rate than our gross national product can support. Thirty-one states presently have a hospital bed occupancy of less than 50 percent. We have excess grain—we export it to those who have less and who wish to buy our grain. We also have an excess capacity in a very fine health care delivery system. We should make this care available to foreign consumers who come from areas of the world where medical care is less developed. We should invite foreign consumers who can afford it to come here and buy our health care. This would raise the level of care they receive, bring cash into the system, and decrease in a favorable manner our balance of trade.

Tough Decisions

Make your thoughts on these issues known to your legislators. Politicians respond to numbers. Informed voters make decisions. Lawmakers respond. We have an obligation to ourselves and to future generations to be informed voters. Stay involved. Keep your mind open with a willingness to learn and share. Create a lifestyle that will stand as a defense to insure your dignity as an individual and as a part of a family, a community, and a nation.

We must study what is at stake in the health care arena today. Medicare, Medicaid, Champus, and soon you will see long-term care, all of these are programs mandated and directed by the government. The issue is: Can the government handle medical programs more cheaply and with greater efficiency than the private sector? Will **access** and **quality** remain?

In conclusion, when you look at our high cost of American medicine, our waste, and our negative financial balance sheet, think also of the many good physicians who have put their lives into restoring others to a productive living. They take the blame for the high cost of heart care. Do they also get the credit for the 23 percent decrease in death from heart disease that has occurred in the United States over the past 15 years? They receive 12.5 percent of the gross national product, but what is it worth when your premature child lives instead of dies, or your seriously ill family member is returned to give you many years of love and is able to work to make this country a better place in which to live? Health care is at the crossroads—Americans must see that it turns in the right direction.

Glossary of Terms

Accrued Benefit: Generally indicates the total benefit earned. Remember, we have no right to these benefits until we are *vested*.

Adjusted Gross Income (AGI): It is item 31 on your 1040 form. It represents our total income for the year less deductions listed in IRC *Section 62*, and before personal exemptions.

Aging: Reduced physiological functions resulting from time, accompanied by a reduced probability of survival.

Allergist: Physician specialist who treats sensitivities to various things, such as animal fur, pollen, foods.

Anesthesiologist: Physician or Registered Nurse specialist whose function is to keep patients from experiencing unreasonable pain during the course of surgical procedures. They are also responsible for monitoring vital signs and administering blood products or fluids during surgery.

Annuity: A guaranteed lifetime income, normally payable on a monthly basis, that may provide income for one or two lives. Payments may terminate upon death of one party, both parties, or after a certain period. Once a payout option has been selected, it can never be changed or altered.

Assignment: An agreement by which a physician accepts a specific charge or fee as payment in full for his or her services.

Beneficiary: A general term for any person who is entitled to receive a benefit. The benefit may be in the form of a monthly check or health care coverage.

Benefit Service: Used in figuring how much money we will receive at retirement.

Break in Service: If we return to work within five years, we must be credited with any years of service before the break in service. The *Retirement Equity Act of 1984* (REA) provided this favorable piece of legislation.

Budgeting: Coordinates our income and expenses. Properly maintained it will clearly indicate how inflation is affecting individual households. It keeps us in touch with how we are spending money.

Cafeteria Plan: Also called flexible benefits and *Section 125* plan. These plans permit employees to select the level of benefits from a package of benefits.

Capitation Payment for Services: Medical services are paid in advance on a per-person basis without knowing whether any service will be required. This prepaid arrangement covers practitioners and hospital services.

Cardiologist: Medical specialist who treats heart disease.

Cash or Deferred Agreement (CODA): refers to a savings program under *Section 401(k)* IRC that enables individuals to save money contributing before tax dollars. The earnings accumulate and compound, tax is deferred.

Coinsurance: Sets forth the percentage of health expenses that you will pay and the percentage that your employer or the health insurance plan will pay. By far the most common coinsurance level is one in which we pay 20 percent of the expenses, and our employer or insurer pays 80 percent. This is also referred to as 80 percent coinsurance.

Compounding: Adding earnings or interest to a capitol base, thereby forming a new and higher base and continuing to add earnings or interest to this new base, etc. The rate of compounding is contingent upon three factors: length of time, amount of money, and the level of earnings.

Contributory Retirement Plan: We and our employer contribute.

Conversion Privilege: A privilege that allows an insured to change to a different plan of insurance offered by the same company, without having to provide evidence of insurability.

Coordination of Benefits (COB): No matter how many policies we may have, this provision limits the total benefits we can collect on each claim to 100 percent of the expenses *covered*. Aimed at cost control to prevent us from receiving duplicate benefits from two or more insurers.

Credited Service: Means the same as vested service.

Custodial Care: Primary personal care, such as housekeeping, cooking, and other duties performed by some health aides.

Cycles in Life: Four important cycles are:

1. **Family cycle—** Periods in our life from birth through childhood, teen years, leaving home, possibly widowhood, and death, which marks the end of our family cycle. Our needs and sources of income will vary with the cycle we are in.
2. **Occupational cycle—** We begin this period with a preparatory phase: grade school, junior high school, high school, perhaps college or trade school, and a career choice is made. We have a period of maximum involvement followed by a phaseout period and finally retirement.
3. **Economic cycle—** Most of us go through an early period of economic dependence, followed by economic independence, and finally, retirement and independence or back to dependence. How well we manage our money during our economic independence phase will determine what we can depend on for income during the last phase of our life.
4. **Age cycle—** This is simply our chronological age cycle.

Deductible: A set dollar amount that we must pay before reimbursement for medical expenses begins.

Deductible Carryover: Permits deductible expenses incurred in the last three months of the prior calendar year (October, November, and December) to be carried over to the new year and counted toward satisfying the new year's deductible.

Defined Benefit Plan: A pension plan that defines the level of monthly income to be provided at retirement. The contributions are actuarially determined in amounts necessary to provide the promised benefit. Employer retains investment risk and the level of benefit guaranteed is advanced funded.

Defined Contribution Plan: Contributions are defined using a formula, and individual accounts are established. Investment results, good or bad, are transferred to the individual participant. Types of defined contribution plans are:

- Individual Retirement Account (IRA)— Sect. 408 IRC
- Money Purchase Plan— Sect. 401(a) IRC
- 401(k)— Salary Reduction Plan
- 403(b)— Tax Shelter Annuity (TSA)
- 457— Deferred Compensation Plan
- Profit-Sharing Plan— Sect. 401(a) IRC.

Dermatologist: Specialist in diseases of the skin.

Diagnosis Related Groups (DRGs): These are categories of illness that determine the amount of money paid to hospitals for treatment of Medicare patients. Currently, there are approximately 500 categories of ailments.

Discrimination: A qualified retirement plan that favors officers, shareholders, or highly compensated employees to the detriment of non-highly compensated employees.

DOL: Department of Labor

Earned Income: Earnings we receive as a return for our labor and services.

Eligible: Probably only means that we are "eligible" to be a participant in the plan. Does not necessarily mean we are eligible to collect a benefit.

Endocrinologist: A specialist in diseases of glands that produce hormones.

Equity Position: The market value of an asset beyond the total amount owed on it.

ERISA: *Employee Retirement Income Security Act of 1974.* The basic law which governs all qualified retirement plans.

Estate Planning: The process of planning how we pass on our accumulated assets to our heirs.

Evidence of Insurability: Proof of our health condition, to determine whether insurance will be granted.

Family Practitioner: A physician who has completed residency training to treat the common medical problems that trouble the average American family member. They are also trained to recognize and refer surgical or medical problems that require specialized treatment.

Fee-for-Service: The health care practitioner or provider is compensated on a piece-work basis as compared to an all-inclusive charge per case.

Fiduciary: A person who holds in trust property or assets to which another has a beneficial interest or title.

Fixed Period Annuity: Fixed periodic payments made for a specified period such as 5 years or 10 years. Payments continue whether the original payee is dead or alive.

Forfeitures: If we terminate our employment before becoming eligible for benefits (vested), then we could lose our benefits.

Gastroenterologist: Specializes in diseases of the stomach and intestines.

General Surgeon: Specialist in abdominal surgery. Some general surgeons have training in neck, vascular, and other types of surgery.

Generation Passing: Deferring the cost for current consumption, by a small segment of a society, to future generations to pay.

Gerontologist: Specialist in diseases of old age.

Gift: A gratuitous transfer of property. This transfer is a gift if it is of a detached and disinterested generosity.

Gynecologist: Specializes in diseases of the female reproductive systems.

Hardship Distribution: May be appropriate in light of immediate and heavy financial needs such as foreclosure on your primary residence or extensive medical bills.

Health Maintenance Organization (HMO): A health care delivery system that provides comprehensive medical care to a voluntarily enrolled population at a predetermined price. As a member we pay a fixed fee (usually monthly) directly to the HMO, for which we receive health care as often as needed.

Hematologist: Medical specialist who treats diseases of the blood.

Home Health Agency: An approved organization that employs skilled persons to deliver medical care in your home.

Hospice: A home-like facility to provide supportive care for the terminally ill and their families.

Individual Retirement Account (IRA): Enables many, whether covered by an employer retirement plan, to save for his or her retirement. IRAs are available only to those with earned income who are under age 70 1/2. Contributions earn tax-deferred interest. The amount contributed may be tax-deductible.

Inflation: An increase in the amount of money in circulation causing a fall in its value and a rise in prices.

Inpatient: A term used to describe being in a hospital or similar medical institution.

Insurance: A system in which several individuals agree to pay a specified amount of money, periodically or in one lump-sum payment, to guarantee that they will be paid if certain conditions and events occur in their lives. The events usually have to do with health, fire, accident, or death of a participant.

Internist: Medical specialist who diagnoses and treats adult patients with medical conditions that do not require surgery.

IRC: Internal Revenue Code

IRS: Internal Revenue Service

Joint and Survivor Annuity: A guaranteed lifetime income that, upon the death of one annuitant, continues to pay some or all of the benefit to the survivor.

Keogh Plan: Also known as HR-10 plan. Available for partnerships and the self-employed. Maximum annual contributions are generally restricted to $30,000.

Kidney Dialysis: A procedure that imitates as closely as possible the functions of the human kidneys and cleans the body of waste. It is performed on people who do not have functioning kidneys.

Lump-Sum Distribution (LSD): A payment made from a qualified retirement plan in one taxable year of the participant, because of death, total disability, attaining age 59 1/2, or separation from service. Participant may be eligible for 5-year or 10-year forward income averaging or long-term capital gains treatment.

Nephrologist: Medical specialist in diseases of the kidneys.

Neurosurgeon: Surgical specialist who operates on the brain and nervous system.

Noncontributory Retirement Plan: Our employer pays the entire cost.

Normal Retirement Age: Age 65 remains the normal retirement age in the United States even though the *Age Discrimination Employment Act* (ADEA) clearly prohibits forcing employees to retire at age 65.

Obstetrician: Specialist who treats women during pregnancy, delivery, and right after childbirth.

Oncologist: Specialist in the medical evaluation and administration of chemotherapy for cancer patients.

Ophthalmologist: Specialist in diseases of the eyes, both medical and surgical.

Orthopedic Surgeon: Specialist who treats diseases of bones, joints, and tendons.

Otorhinolaryngologist: Specialist in disease of the ear, nose, and throat (ENT).

Outpatient: Services given by a hospital to a person who has *not* been admitted to the hospital.

Participant: We are covered in the plan though not assured of collecting a pension.

Pay-as-you-go: A system of paying for a benefit out of current cash flow.

PBGC: Pension Benefit Guarantee Corporation. A non-profit organization created by ERISA-1974, responsible for insuring defined benefit pension plans. Corporate defined benefit plans pay an annual insurance premium for each covered employee, terminated vested employee, and retired employee. This federal agency is experiencing financial difficulty.

Pediatrician: Specialist in childhood development and children's diseases.

Perception: The process by which an individual organizes and interprets data received through the sensory systems of the body.

Plastic Surgeon: Specialist who operates to improve looks or to repair appearance after an accident. Many plastic surgeons specialize in the reconstruction process for burn patients.

Preferred Provider Organization (PPO): An arrangement with a group of medical care providers who agree to provide services at negotiated fees in return for prompt and timely payment and a guaranteed patient volume.

Psychiatrist: Treats mental and emotional problems.

Qualified Plan: A defined benefit or defined contribution plan that permits tax advantages for employers and employees.

Radiologist: An expert in x-rays and other rays for diagnosis and treatment.

Recipient: A person who receives public assistance or welfare payments. This is distinguished from a beneficiary, who buys or pays for protection by working in covered employment and paying Social Security taxes.

Retirement Income: Income that flows into our household from all sources, once we cease working and earned income stops.

Rheumatologist: Medical specialist in joint diseases and arthritis.

Rollover Account: Refers to a transfer of retirement funds from one qualified plan to another. If the participant takes constructive receipt of the funds he or she has 60 days in which to deposit the funds into another qualified plan. Failure to make this deposit in the prescribed time frame can result in substantial penalties if the participant has not attained age 59 1/2.

Second Opinion: Usually refers to surgery and is a cost-control vehicle to reduce unnecessary surgery by encouraging individuals to seek an evaluation by another physician before accepting elective surgery.

Single Life Annuity: Guarantees income for one life only for his or her lifetime.

Skilled Nursing Facility: A facility that provides skilled nursing care, rehabilitation services, and other related health care services.

Social Security: A federal program. The technical title is the Old-Age Survivors, Disability, and Health Insurance System (OASDI). Participants are those who pay into the system during their working years, their spouse, and dependents. Benefits vary according to earnings, duration of payments into the program, and age.

Social Security Integration: There are two general types of integration:

1. Subtracts part of our Social Security benefit from our pension benefit; and
2. Credits only earnings above a certain amount.

Stop Loss/Maximum Out-Of-Pocket (MOOP): The maximum that we will have to pay for expenses covered under our plan. The most common MOOP is $1,000 - $2,500. These maximums are increasing frequently. All expenses in excess of MOOP are paid by the insurer. If our coinsurance obligation exceeds the MOOP limit, our expense would be limited to the MOOP. Therefore, the MOOP puts a cap on the cost of a catastrophic illness.

Summary Plan Description (SPD): Contains specific information about our benefit plans. The *Employee Retirement Income Security Act of 1974* (ERISA) requires that we be provided a SPD if we are a participant in a plan. The Department of Labor is also required to receive a copy from our employer.

Tax-Sheltered Annuity (TSA): Is a deferred tax arrangement under *Section 403(b)* of the IRC. The plan may be used only for organizations structured under *Section 501(c)(3)* of the tax code, or a public school system. Salary deferral can generally be 20 percent of income or $9,500 per year, whichever is less.

Third-Party Administrator (TPA): Refers to a person or organization that provides certain administrative services to a group benefits plan, including premium accounting, claim review and payment, COBRA administration, individual stop loss records, aggregate stop loss records, case management, claims utilization review, maintenance of employee eligibility records, and negotiations with insurers that provide stop loss protection for large claims.

Thoracic Surgeon: Specialist who treats diseases of the heart, lung, esophagus, and chest when surgery is required.

Time Value of Money: This is the opportunity cost of money. If we expend our money in a particular use, the opportunity cost is the earning power the money would have had if we had used it in other ways.

Trust: Creates a relationship where one person, the trustee, is the owner of title to property, and is subject to obligations to keep and use the property for the benefit of another, called the beneficiary or beneficiaries.

Unearned Income: Money received as a result of having money working for us. It can flow to us as a result of money deposited in a credit union, bank, mutual fund, money market fund, or savings and loan organization, or other invested assets.

Urologist: Specialist in problems of the urinary tract and male reproductive system.

Variable Annuity: Monthly income may vary according to changes in cost of living or investment results.

Vested: Some pension benefits will be ours at retirement, even if we should leave the company before our retirement date.

Vested Service: The years our plan requires in determining whether we have worked long enough to have a vested right to receive a pension.

Will: A written document proclaiming how our accumulated assets are to be distributed at death.

Will Substitute: When we name a beneficiary on such plans as life insurance, pensions, profit sharing, individual retirement accounts, and property held in joint tenancy, the individuals so named will receive benefits when we die. The above designations will substitute regardless what our will may contain.

Year of Service: We are credited with a year of service if during a 12-month period we work at least 1,000 hours.

References

Ball, R. *Social Security: Today and Tomorrow*. New York, Columbia University Press, 1978.

Burrough, B. & Helyar, J. *Barbarians At The Gate*. New York, Harper Perennial, 1991.

Collins, T. *The Complete Guide to Retirement*. Englewood Cliffs, N.J., Prentice-Hall, 1977.

Davidson, J., *The Squeeze*. New York, Summit Books, 1980.

"Death Rate in LA Fell in Slowdown by Doctors." *The Washington Post*, October 20, 1978.

Drucker, P., *Innovation & Entrepreneurship: Practice & Principles*. New York: Harper & Row, 1985.

Financial Accounting Standards Board, *Statement of Financial Accounting Standards No. 106*. Financial Accounting Foundation, 1990.

Ideas for Retirees. Englewood Cliffs, N.J., Prentice-Hall, 1981.

Kaplan, L. *Retiring Right: Planning for Your Successful Retirement.* Wayne, N.J., Avery Publishing Group, Inc., 1987.

Report of the Special Trustee Joint Committee, *TIAA-CREF: The Future Agenda,* New York, TIAA-CREF, 1987.

Sahin, I., *Health Care Benefits for Retirees: A Framework for Measurement.* International Foundation of Employee Benefit Plans, 1988.

Simon, W. *A Time for Truth.* McGraw-Hill Book Company, New York, 1978.

Strauss, W. & Howe, N., *Generations.* New York, William Morrow and Company, Inc., 1991.

U.S. Department of Health and Human Services, Pension and Welfare Benefit Programs, *Estimating Your Social Security Retirement Check: Using the Indexing Method.* Washington D.C., 1974.

U.S. Department of Health and Human Services, *When You Get Social Security Retirement or Survivors Benefits.* Social Security Administration, 1991.

U.S. Department of Labor, *Employer's Pension Guide.* Pension Benefit Guaranty Corporation, 1990.

U.S. Department of Labor, *Opportunity 2000: Creative Affirmation Action Strategies for a Changing Work Force.* Washington D.C., 1988.

U.S. Department of Labor, *Three Budgets for a Retired Couple.* Bureau of Labor Statistics, Washington D.C.: Periodic.

U.S. Department of Labor, *What You Should Know About the Pension Law.* U.S. Government Printing Office, 1990.

Index

W

About the Publisher

PROBUS PUBLISHING COMPANY

Probus Publishing Company fills the informational needs of today's business professional by publishing authoritative, quality books on timely and relevant topics, including:

- Investing
- Futures/Options Trading
- Banking
- Finance
- Marketing and Sales
- Manufacturing and Project Management
- Personal Finance, Real Estate, Insurance and Estate Planning
- Entrepreneurship
- Management

Probus books are available at quantity discounts when purchased for business, educational or sales promotional use. For more information, please call the Director, Corporate/Institutional Sales at 1-800-PROBUS-1, or write:

Director, Corporate/Institutional Sales
Probus Publishing Company
1925 N. Clybourn Avenue
Chicago, Illinois 60614
FAX (312) 868-6250